9-95

The Guide Association

KNOT
BOOK

THE GUIDE
ASSOCIATION

The Guide Association Knot Book
Written by: Wendy Goodhind
With thanks to Shaun Lacey and Chris Raworth
Project Editor: Clare Jefferis
Editors: Kathryn Cleary and Helen Sutcliffe
Designer: Gillian Webb
Illustrator: Wendy Hesse

Printed and bound in England by The Lavenham Press

ISBN 0 85260 146 8

Published by The Guide Association
17–19 Buckingham Palace Road
London SW1W 0PT
E-mail: chq@guides.org.uk
Web site: http://www.guides.org.uk
The Guide Association Trading Service ordering code 60723

Members are reminded that during the life span of this publication policy
changes may be made by The Guide Association which will affect the accuracy
of information within these pages.

Grandpa Knot and Pedigree Cow Hitch reproduced with kind permission of
Robert, Pauline and Katherine Asher.

Pioneering projects: Swing Bridge or Haymaker Bridge, Rope Ladder, 'A' Frame Transporter,
Swing or Trapeze, Swingboat, See-Saw, Raft and Monkey Bridge or Burmah Bridge reproduced
with kind permission of Edith Chadwick and Pauline McKie.

Skylon pioneering project reproduced with kind permission of
Oxfordshire Pioneering Team.

The pioneering projects in this book have all been tried and tested.
We believe the information given is accurate and the designs safe.
No responsibility can be accepted should this prove incorrect.

Contents

continued...

Foreword

Knotting is a skill that has been part of our heritage for hundreds of years. It is a skill that is still used in many practical ways, in gardening, in sailing and in the rescue services. You can see evidence of the craft in clothes and furnishings and in designs on jewellery and decorations on ancient stones. In fact, knots are a part of everyday life. Start looking and you will find them everywhere – from tying your shoelaces to putting a luggage label on your suitcase. They have even found their way into university maths courses!

From the start of Guiding knot tying has been a traditional activity and even now, every time that you, as a Brownie, Guide, Senior Section member or adult, make a friendship bracelet, put up a tent or learn to abseil, you make use of the skills of knotting.

This book makes it easy for you to learn even complicated knots and once you have practised them you will be able to make and do some amazing things. So take a length of string or rope and get started...

I know you'll enjoy it.

Elizabeth M. Ferrier

Elizabeth M Ferrier
Chairman of Programme and Training Committee

Introduction

E veryone uses knots, but many people don't know how to tie more than two or three. Knots *are* useful! This book will help you develop your knotting skills whatever your experience. It includes the knots needed for all stages of the Association's Knotter badge and other interest badges and pennants, plus those needed throughout the programme, whether it is first aid, craft, camping, or other outdoor activities.

   As you advance you will find that many knots are related. From one basic knot many more complicated knots can develop, for example a simple Overhand Knot can advance to a Square Shoestring knot in only a few steps.

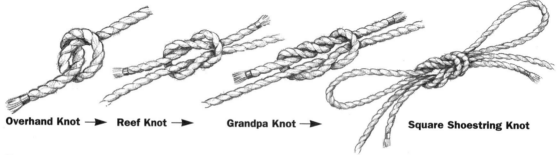

Overhand Knot ➔ **Reef Knot** ➔   **Grandpa Knot** ➔   **Square Shoestring Knot**

Each knot is explained in easy stages with clear pictures showing each step. This should allow you to teach yourself any knot you need.

Practise makes perfect

We all learn how to tie knots in different ways, but start simply and build up your skill.
- At first practise using cord. Get a 'feel' for tying the knots and then use other ropes.
- A length of cord takes up almost no room – so carry a piece with you so you can practise anywhere!
- Use two pieces of cord of equal thickness and in contrasting colours. This allows you to see at a glance the route each cord takes.
- Some of the gadgets and pioneering projects need to be tackled in a group – so make that diary date!
- Practise the knotting tricks in front of a friend before performing in public. Follow the diagrams carefully, so it genuinely looks like magic!

The language of knotting

Knotting, like many other skills, has its own vocabulary. Try to familiarise yourself with some of these terms so that you can follow the steps easily.

A length of rope has two ends:

- The **working** end – the end you hold and tie the knot with.
- The **standing** end – the fixed or non-moving end, which might already be tied to another object.
- The **bight** is the length between the two ends or a bend in the rope. Some knots are tied 'in the bight' which means they are tied without using either end.

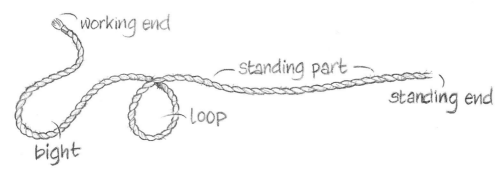

- The term **standing part** refers to the length of bight between the standing end and the knot.
- A **loop** is a much tighter bend in the cord than a bight. It can be an open loop with the ends apart or a closed loop with the ends crossed.

These terms and others are used throughout the book. You will soon get used to them, but wherever you come across a word or phrase you don't understand, turn to the Glossary on page 142.

Knots and their uses

A knot refers to anything that is deliberately tied in a cord or rope. Which knot you choose depends on the task it has to perform. Traditionally knots are grouped into categories according to their uses. The following common knotting terms are useful to know:

- **Hitches** – knots that fasten a rope to another object, e.g. a pole.

continued...

- Bends – knots that join two ropes or cords.
- Splices – knots that secure two ropes or two parts of a rope by interweaving the strands.
- Sennits – decorative knots or plaitings.
  In addition there are:
- Whippings – that bind the end of a rope to prevent fraying.
- Lashings – that fasten or bind two poles together.

You need only master a few knots from each of these categories to be able to perform tricks, make gadgets or assemble pioneering projects, e.g. once you can tie Square Lashing, West Country Whipping and a Clove Hitch you can make a basic flagpole.

Choosing your materials

The materials you choose are important and must be suitable for the task. Here are some examples of materials and their uses:
- String, which is thin and often used for tying up parcels.
- Cord, which is thicker than string, is great for learning how to tie knots. It is also used for many decorative knots such as woggles.
- Nylon rope is very strong and used for rock climbing and mountaineering.
- Hemp rope is strong and grips well but can be stiff. It is ideal for pioneering projects.
- Polypropylene is not as strong as hemp but it does float. This means it is ideal for water activities.

Safety

Safety is a vital concern when using knots and ropes in practical situations.
Here are some good safety tips to remember:
- Respect ropes and knots – never put yourself or anyone else in a situation where the movement or tightening of the rope might do harm.
- Put your materials (rope, string, cord, etc) away when you are not using them even if it is only for a short time.
- Use the right knot for the right task. If you are not sure whether it is right, check with someone who knows.
- If you do need to release someone from a rope, sever the cord and not the knot as this may be needed for evidence.
- Never put a rope around your own or someone else's neck.

Knots

Thumb Knot or Overhand Knot

It is the simplest knot there is and you have probably been able to tie it for years without knowing its name. It is used as a stopper knot, e.g. between beads on a necklace or at the end of a sewing thread or, in an emergency, to stop a rope from fraying.

1 Place the working end over the standing part to form a closed loop.

2 Take the working end through the loop.

3 Pull on both ends to tighten knot. Loops can be overhand or underhand.

Double Overhand Knot

T he Double Overhand Knot forms a simple but firm loop in the end or middle of a rope, e.g. at the end of a skipping rope to form hand loops.

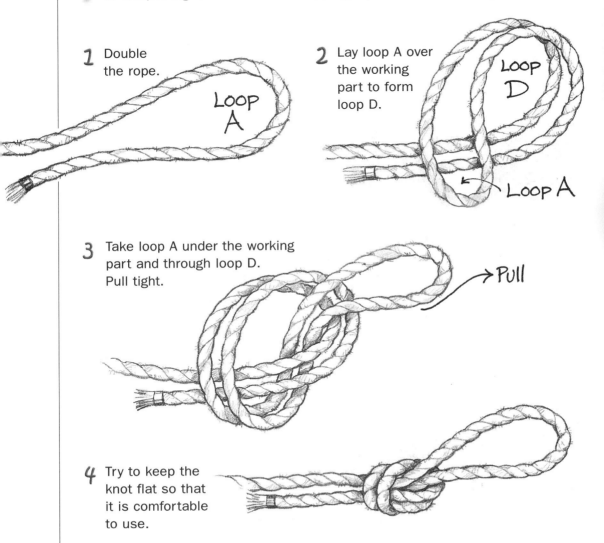

1 Double the rope.

LOOP A

2 Lay loop A over the working part to form loop D.

LOOP D

LOOP A

3 Take loop A under the working part and through loop D. Pull tight.

→ Pull

4 Try to keep the knot flat so that it is comfortable to use.

Figure-of-Eight Knot

This is a more secure and chunky knot than the Thumb Knot (see page 10) and is easier to untie. It is used as a stopper knot or as a decorative knot at the end of a weave.

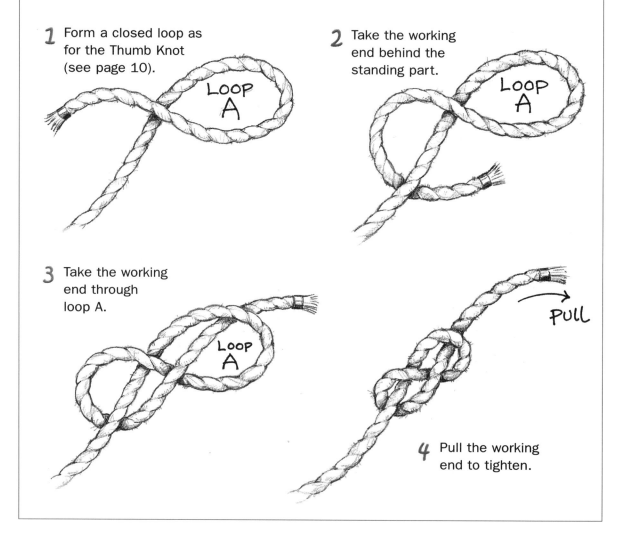

1 Form a closed loop as for the Thumb Knot (see page 10).

LOOP A

2 Take the working end behind the standing part.

LOOP A

3 Take the working end through loop A.

LOOP A

PULL

4 Pull the working end to tighten.

Packer's Knot

B ased on the Figure-of-Eight Knot the Packers Knot, as its name suggests, is excellent for tying up parcels. It is a slip knot and so can be put into position and pulled tight.

1 Pass string around the parcel. Take the working end behind the standing end.

2 Pass the working end back over itself to form a closed loop. Then bring the working end under itself.

3 Pass the working end through the loop and pull tight.

pull

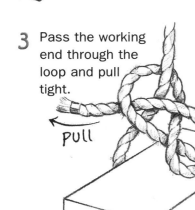

4 Pull the standing end until it locks before finishing tying the parcel.

pull

13

Reef Knot and Release

This binding knot is generally tied using both ends of the same length of rope. Tied to itself with equal pressure from both directions it is a useful and secure knot. With uneven pressure or movement it will easily become unfastened and soon slide apart if tied to another rope of a different thickness.

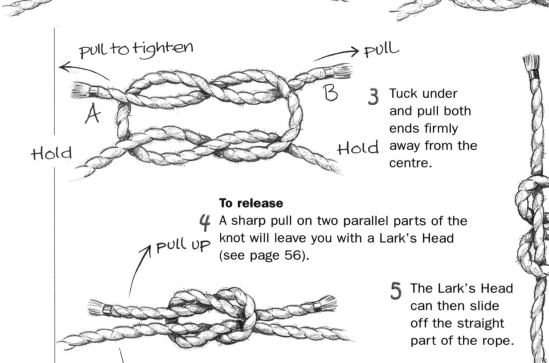

1 Take each end of a piece of rope in each hand. Place the left end over the right and tuck under.

B

A

2 Now place end A over end B.

A   B

pull to tighten

pull

B

A

Hold   Hold

3 Tuck under and pull both ends firmly away from the centre.

To release

4 A sharp pull on two parallel parts of the knot will leave you with a Lark's Head (see page 56).

Pull up

5 The Lark's Head can then slide off the straight part of the rope.

pull down

14

Granny Knot

The Granny Knot does not stay tied for very long and will jam under strain. It should not be used for any purpose other than tricks. However, it is important to recognise this knot as it is frequently tied by mistake.

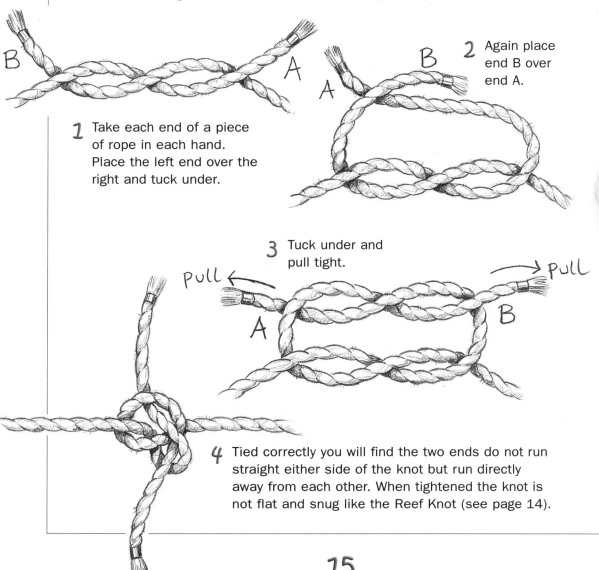

1 Take each end of a piece of rope in each hand. Place the left end over the right and tuck under.

2 Again place end B over end A.

3 Tuck under and pull tight.

4 Tied correctly you will find the two ends do not run straight either side of the knot but run directly away from each other. When tightened the knot is not flat and snug like the Reef Knot (see page 14).

Surgeon's Reef Knot

This knot is used in fine, nylon thread when an extra twist is needed to hold the knot together. It is not bulky and lies flat like the Reef Knot (see page 14).

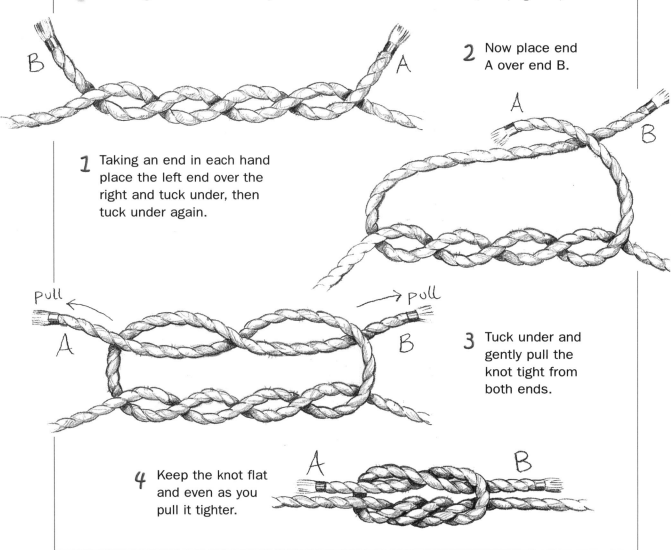

1 Taking an end in each hand place the left end over the right and tuck under, then tuck under again.

2 Now place end A over end B.

3 Tuck under and gently pull the knot tight from both ends.

4 Keep the knot flat and even as you pull it tighter.

Grandpa Knot

The Grandpa Knot is a new knot created by Harry Asher. It is similar to the Surgeon's Reef Knot (see page 16).

1 With an end in each hand place the left end over the right and tuck under.

2 Now place end A over end B.

3 Tuck under and then under again.

4 Pull firmly to tighten the knot.

Reef Bow & Release

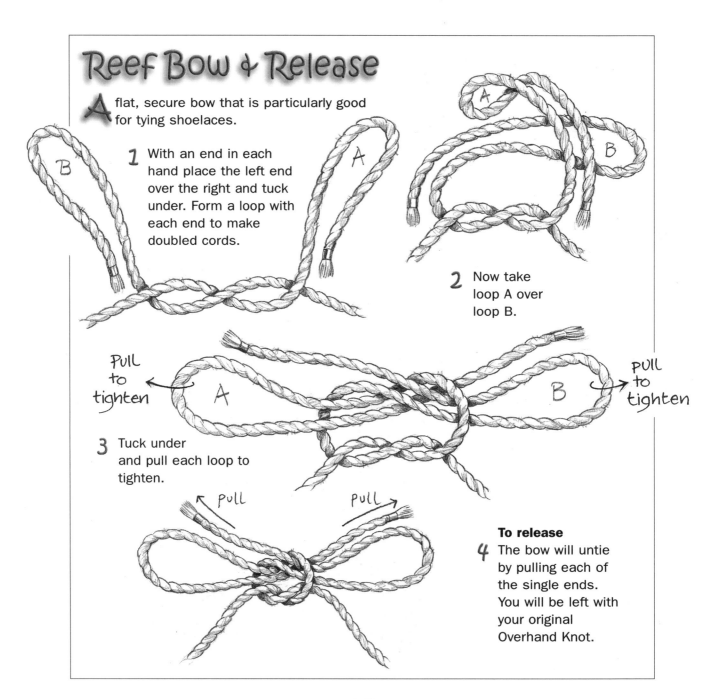

A flat, secure bow that is particularly good for tying shoelaces.

1 With an end in each hand place the left end over the right and tuck under. Form a loop with each end to make doubled cords.

2 Now take loop A over loop B.

Pull to tighten

Pull to tighten

3 Tuck under and pull each loop to tighten.

Pull

Pull

To release

4 The bow will untie by pulling each of the single ends. You will be left with your original Overhand Knot.

18

Square Shoestring Knot & Release

This is a very secure bow that is useful for tying shoelaces that insist on coming undone – a quality knot for super knotters!

1 Double the cords. Holding a loop in each hand place the left loop over the right.

2 Tuck loop A under loop B.

3 Then place loop A over loop B and tuck under. Pull the loops to tighten.

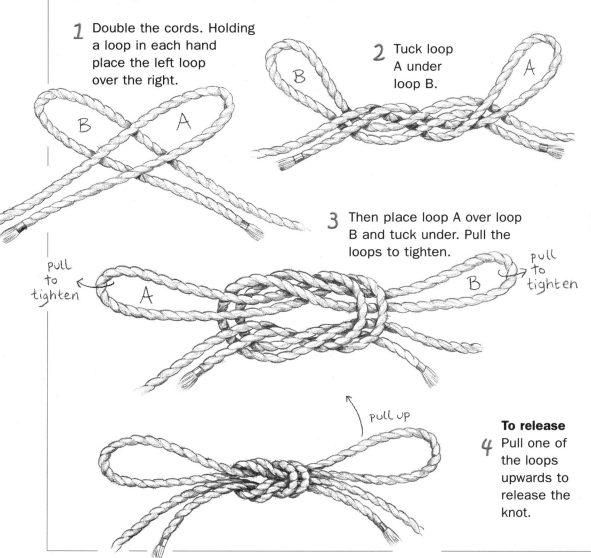

pull to tighten

pull to tighten

pull up

To release

4 Pull one of the loops upwards to release the knot.

Bowline with Stopper Knot

A Bowline is a very secure knot which is used to form a loop. It is a knot which will not slip or easily come untied. It is commonly used in mountaineering for tying on at the end of a rope.

1 Form a loop and hold it in place at X.

2 Pass end B up through the loop forming a second larger loop.

3 Now take end B behind A and back down through the first loop.

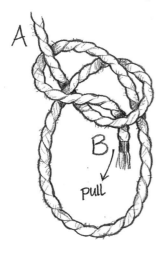

4 Tighten the knot to adjust the size of the larger loop formed.

5 Using end B, place a Thumb Knot (see page 10) round the larger loop as a stopper knot for added security.

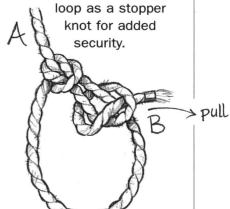

Slip Knot

This makes a simple loop which can be used to slip over a pole.

1 Form a closed loop.

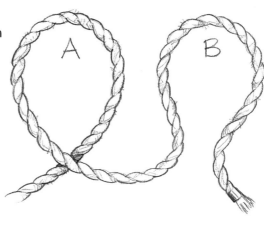

2 Form an open loop in the working end.

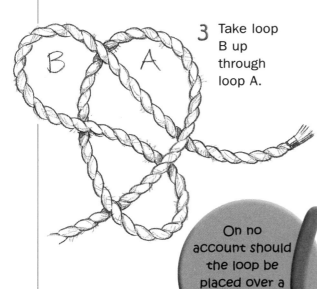

3 Take loop B up through loop A.

4 Slip loop B over the post. Tighten the knot by pulling on the standing end. Tighten the loop by pulling on the working end.

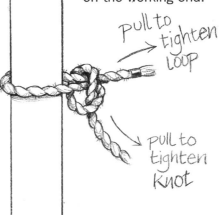

pull to tighten loop

pull to tighten knot

On no account should the loop be placed over a person's head or neck.

21

Hand Knot

A firm joining knot which is made in two parallel cords. The Hand Knot is a neat and flat knot.

1 Make a Figure-of-Eight Knot (see page 12) with cord A.

2 Take cord B. Going from the working end of cord A, follow the line of the Figure-of-Eight Knot.

3 When complete, the working ends of cords A and B should be at opposite sides. Tighten by working the two ends – keeping the knot flat throughout.

Hitches

Single & Half Hitches

These are the two basic hitches and are usually formed as part of more complex hitches. They will hold on their own as long as the pressure remains on the standing end.

Single Hitch

1 Pass the cord over a pole.

2 Bring the working end round the pole and tuck under the working part. Pressure from the standing end holds the hitch in place – but not very securely!

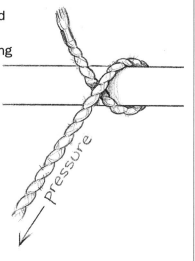

Half Hitch

1 Pass the cord over a pole. Then bring the working end in front and then behind the standing part. Take the working end up through loop A.

Round Turn & Two Half Hitches

A good method for fastening a cord to a pole or post when the pressure remains constant on the standing end, e.g. when putting up a washing line.

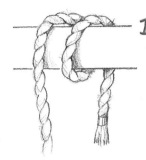

1 A Round Turn is formed when a cord is placed around a pole twice.

2 The two Half Hitches secure the turn. Take the working end in front, then round behind the standing part and up through loop A. Repeat to form a second hitch.

3 Close the hitches by pulling on the working end as each hitch is completed. Pressure on the standing part will tighten the hitch.

PULL

Fisherman's Bend

This is one of the strongest hitches, but is infact called a bend. It gets its name from the traditional language of seamen and is used to make fast a rope to an anchor or spar.

1 Form a Round Turn around a spar. Take the working end in front of the standing part and behind the two turns. Pull on the working end to tighten the hitch.

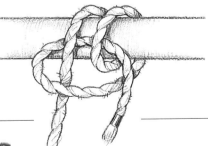

25

Figure-of-Eight Hitch

Although this is more secure than the simple Half Hitch (see page 24), it will not take a great deal of pressure and is best used as a temporary hitch.

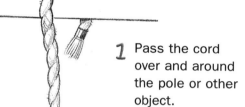

1 Pass the cord over and around the pole or other object.

2 Bring the working end in front of the standing part and then pass it around the back of the standing part.

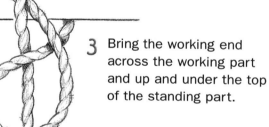

3 Bring the working end across the working part and up and under the top of the standing part.

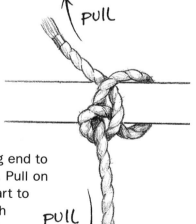

4 Pull the working end to close the hitch. Pull on the standing part to tighten the hitch around the pole.

26

Slipped Hitch

This hitch is not very secure in itself but is used in a number of other hitches or as a series of interlocking Slipped Hitches. It has the advantage of releasing quickly which is useful for brailing up tent doors.

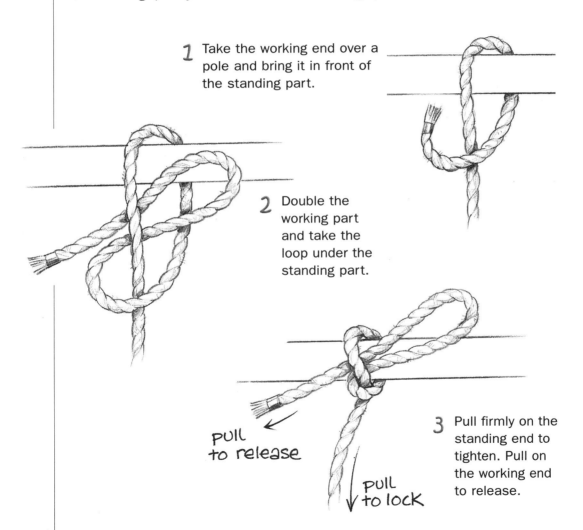

1 Take the working end over a pole and bring it in front of the standing part.

2 Double the working part and take the loop under the standing part.

PULL to release

PULL to lock

3 Pull firmly on the standing end to tighten. Pull on the working end to release.

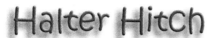

Halter Hitch

This is an easy, general-purpose hitch which readily unties. It is useful for brailing when the cords are smooth and the hitch needs to be secure. It may be used for tying up horses.

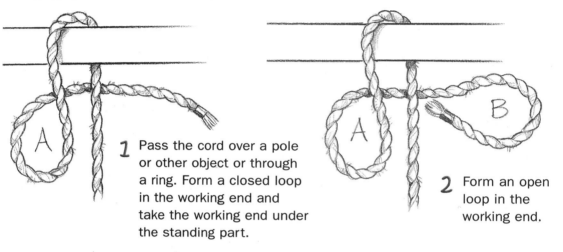

1 Pass the cord over a pole or other object or through a ring. Form a closed loop in the working end and take the working end under the standing part.

2 Form an open loop in the working end.

3 Take loop B over the standing part and through loop A. Pull on the standing end to tighten.

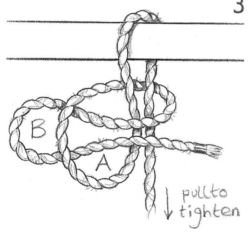

pull to tighten

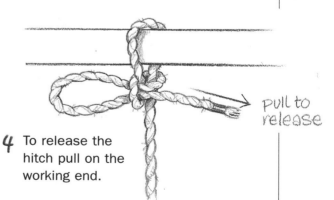

pull to release

4 To release the hitch pull on the working end.

Donkey Hitch or Quick Release Knot

The Donkey Hitch can be used to tie up brailings or the door on a tent. On a tent wall or door both the cord ends will be stitched in place.

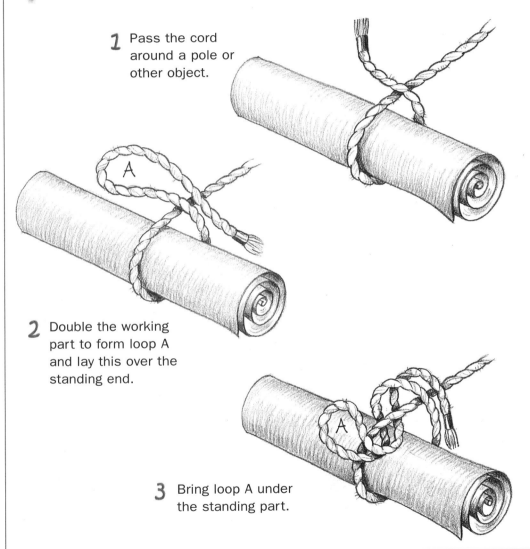

1 Pass the cord around a pole or other object.

2 Double the working part to form loop A and lay this over the standing end.

3 Bring loop A under the standing part.

continued...

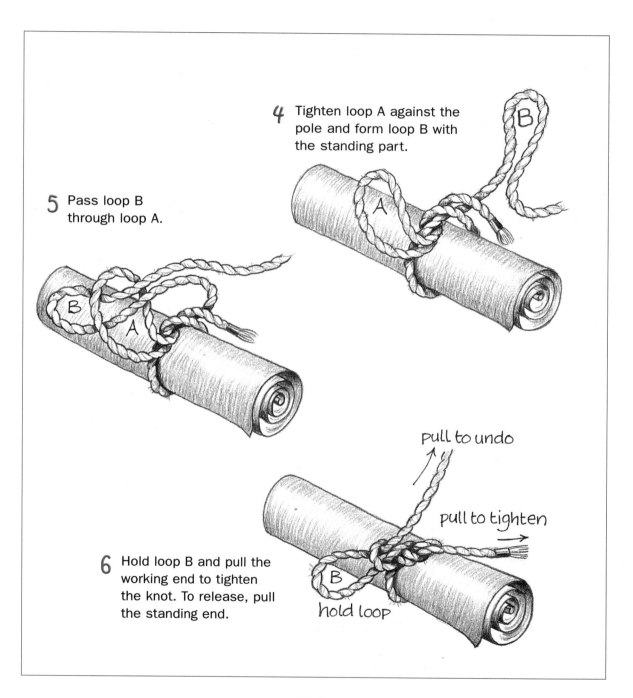

4 Tighten loop A against the pole and form loop B with the standing part.

5 Pass loop B through loop A.

6 Hold loop B and pull the working end to tighten the knot. To release, pull the standing end.

pull to undo

pull to tighten

hold loop

Highwayman's Hitch

This is a very secure hitch that can be used to tie up an animal or moving object, e.g. a raft. Why not tell a get-away-quick story such as Dick Turpin and his horse Black Bess when you are teaching younger children how to tie this knot?

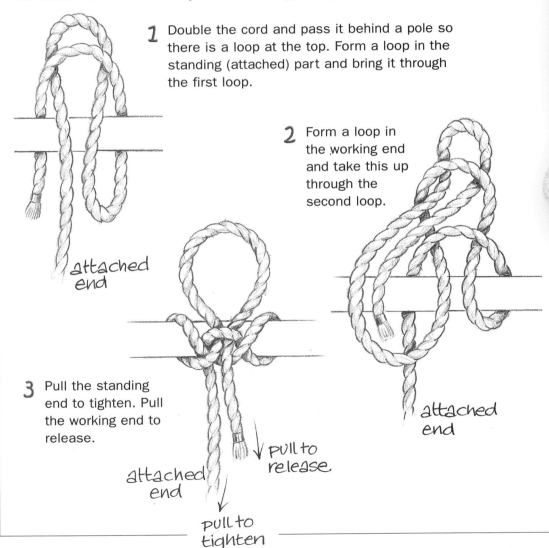

1 Double the cord and pass it behind a pole so there is a loop at the top. Form a loop in the standing (attached) part and bring it through the first loop.

2 Form a loop in the working end and take this up through the second loop.

attached end

3 Pull the standing end to tighten. Pull the working end to release.

attached end

pull to release

attached end

pull to tighten

attached end

Timber Hitch

A hitch to hold together logs or poles temporarily, e.g. when bringing a bundle of firewood to the campsite. The wood can be of different shapes or sizes as the pull from the standing end draws everything together. This hitch pulls apart quite easily so it is good to use when your cord may get wet, e.g. when towing poles across water.

1 Lay the cord flat and place the bundle on top of the cord. Take the working end and form a Half Hitch (see page 24) round the standing part of the cord.

2 Wrap the working end around the working part two or three times.

3 Pull the standing end to tighten. Where the wood does not fit easily together, jerk the standing end two or three times to tighten the cord around the bundle.

PULL

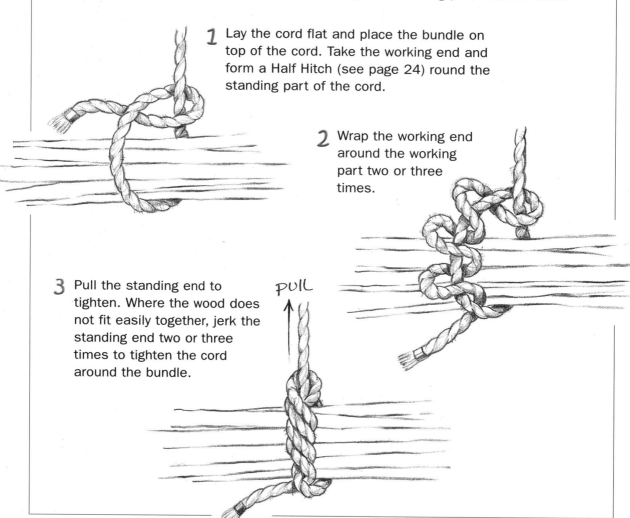

32

Killick Hitch

A Timber Hitch (see page 32) with a Single Hitch (see page 24) further along the balance is called a Killick Hitch. It is used to balance a bundle particularly when it contains long pieces of wood or spars.

1 Complete the Timber Hitch as on page 32.

2 Take the standing end and tie a Single Hitch (see page 24) further along your bundle so that it is securely balanced.

Pole Hitch or Tent-Pole Hitch

U sed to fasten tent-poles firmly together for transportation or storage. This hitch appears to be unique to The Guide Association!

1 Place the cord in an 'S' shape. Lay the bundle of poles across the cord. You now have two working ends and two loops.

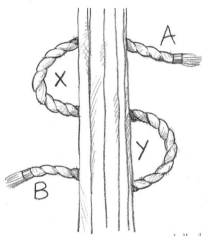

2 Take end A across the bundle and through loop X. Take end B across the bundle and through loop Y.

3 Close up the two parts. Pull both working ends tightly, if necessary moving the poles so that they fit snugly together. Tie a Reef Knot (see page 14) with ends A and B.

4 To hold the hitch firmly in place pull both working ends tightly.

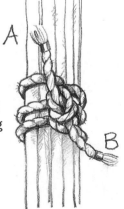

Cow Hitch

Although this is not a very secure hitch, it can be useful if there is equal pull on both ends of the rope. It is doubtful whether anyone uses it to tie up a cow!

1 Double the cord.

2 Bring the closed end down over the cords.

3 Slide the two loops you have created over a post or pole.

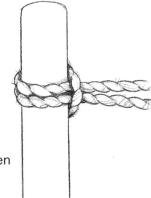

4 Pull the two ends to tighten the hitch.

Pedigree Cow Hitch

This version of the Cow Hitch was created by Harry Asher. It is more secure than the plain Cow Hitch (see page 35).

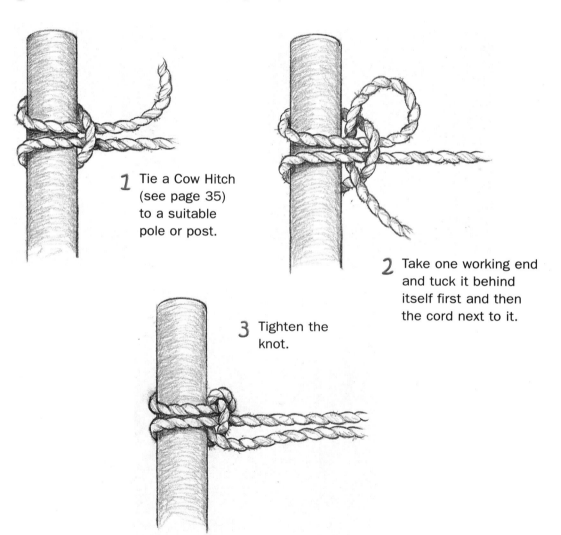

1 Tie a Cow Hitch (see page 35) to a suitable pole or post.

2 Take one working end and tuck it behind itself first and then the cord next to it.

3 Tighten the knot.

Clove Hitch

Of the many hitches this is probably the most commonly used. The Clove Hitch is very old and is used both on land and at sea. Despite this, it is not the most secure of hitches and, if used without additional hitches, needs pressure on both ends to keep it secure. However, the Clove Hitch is the basis for many other knots.

There are a number of ways of tying the Clove Hitch. Circumstances will in part determine the method you use, but you may generally prefer a particular method.

Method A

Use this method when both ends of a pole are closed off or if you are using a ring.

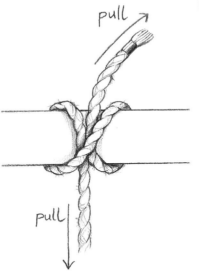

1 Take the cord and pass the working end round the pole and across the standing part.

2 Pass the working end back over the pole and then take it through itself. The two cords out of the hitch now lie in opposite directions.

3 Pull both cords to tighten the hitch.

continued...

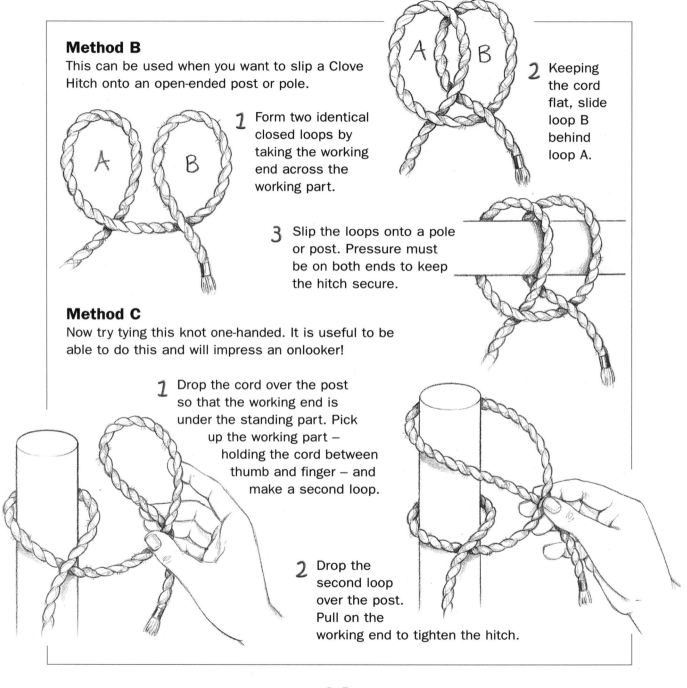

Method B

This can be used when you want to slip a Clove Hitch onto an open-ended post or pole.

1 Form two identical closed loops by taking the working end across the working part.

2 Keeping the cord flat, slide loop B behind loop A.

3 Slip the loops onto a pole or post. Pressure must be on both ends to keep the hitch secure.

Method C

Now try tying this knot one-handed. It is useful to be able to do this and will impress an onlooker!

1 Drop the cord over the post so that the working end is under the standing part. Pick up the working part – holding the cord between thumb and finger – and make a second loop.

2 Drop the second loop over the post. Pull on the working end to tighten the hitch.

38

Rolling Hitch or Magnus Hitch

This hitch has been used by Sailors for generations to attach a thin line to a heavier rope and is designed to take a lengthwise pull or strain. You must work out from which direction the pull will come and tie the hitch so that the double turn is on the side that will take the strain.

1 Take the cord over the heavier rope.

2 Take the working end across the working part and round the heavier rope twice.

3 Take the working end under the second turn and pull to tighten the hitch.

pull to tighten

direction of strain

4 The illustration (below) shows the hitch taking the strain from the other direction.

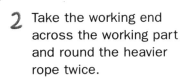

pull to tighten

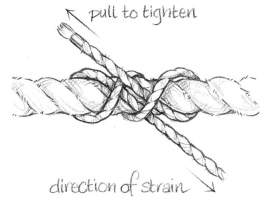

direction of strain

Chair Knot

The Chair Knot is used to lower or raise a person vertically only in an extreme emergency. The person who is doing the lowering must be capable of taking the weight of the person being lowered and understand how to protect themselves.

　　The person being lowered may be able to co-operate if conscious, but otherwise she or he will be floppy, heavy and difficult to put into the 'chair' safely. Practice tying the knot and putting it under pressure in a safe situation so that you are able to use it confidently should you have no alternative.

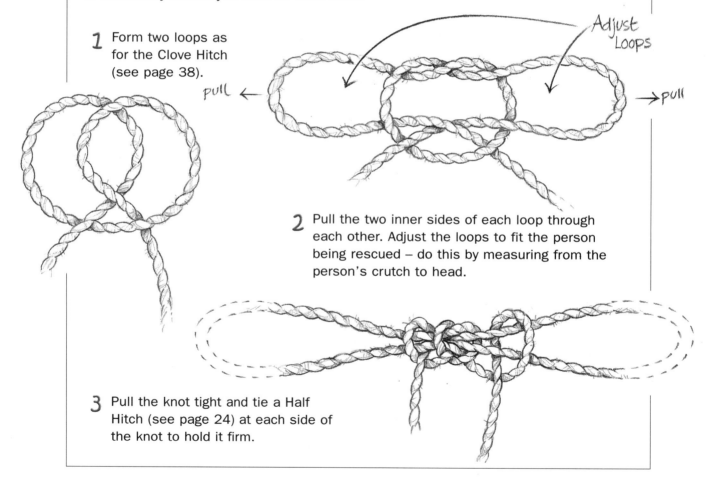

1 Form two loops as for the Clove Hitch (see page 38).

Adjust LOOPS

pull ←　　　　　　　　　→ pull

2 Pull the two inner sides of each loop through each other. Adjust the loops to fit the person being rescued – do this by measuring from the person's crutch to head.

3 Pull the knot tight and tie a Half Hitch (see page 24) at each side of the knot to hold it firm.

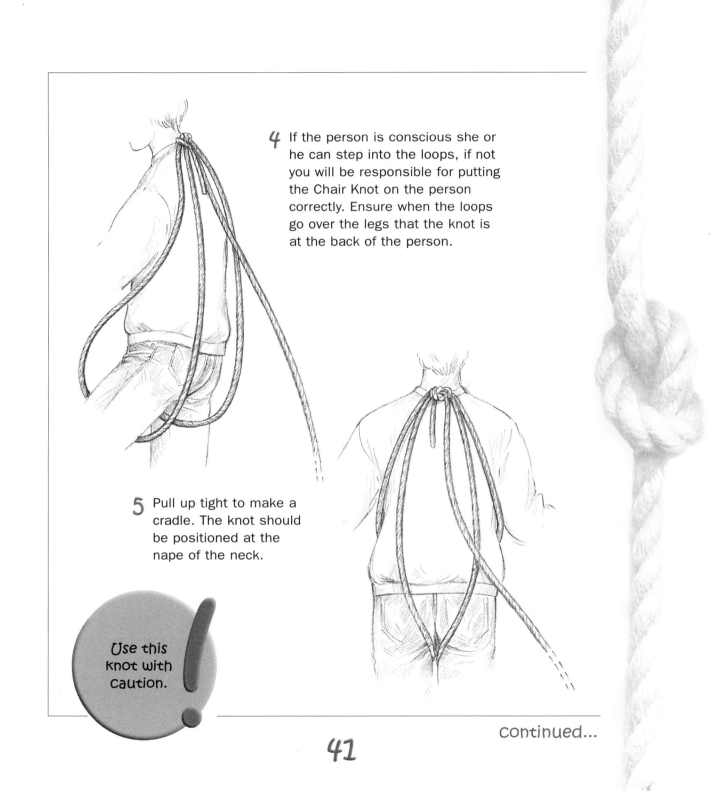

4 If the person is conscious she or
   he can step into the loops, if not
   you will be responsible for putting
   the Chair Knot on the person
   correctly. Ensure when the loops
   go over the legs that the knot is
   at the back of the person.

5 Pull up tight to make a
   cradle. The knot should
   be positioned at the
   nape of the neck.

Use this
knot with
caution.

41

continued...

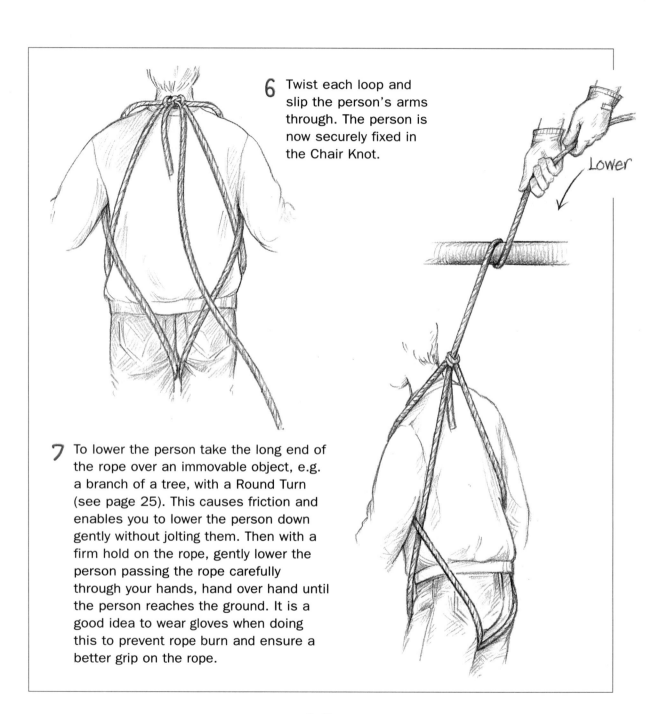

6 Twist each loop and slip the person's arms through. The person is now securely fixed in the Chair Knot.

Lower

7 To lower the person take the long end of the rope over an immovable object, e.g. a branch of a tree, with a Round Turn (see page 25). This causes friction and enables you to lower the person down gently without jolting them. Then with a firm hold on the rope, gently lower the person passing the rope carefully through your hands, hand over hand until the person reaches the ground. It is a good idea to wear gloves when doing this to prevent rope burn and ensure a better grip on the rope.

Sheepshank

The Sheepshank is often used to reduce the length of a cord without cutting and joining. It can also be used to strengthen a portion of cord which has become weakened as a single strand, the pressure being transferred to the hitch. To keep it in place the hitches need to be under pressure and the knot must be carefully adjusted. If your Sheepshank is tied outdoors it will be affected by the weather and will need to be adjusted as it slackens or tightens. In windy conditions or if your rope is very stiff, the Sheepshank can be strengthened by placing two toggles or two pieces of wood through the loops.

The Sheepshank belongs to the Clove Hitch family (see page 37) and there are three ways of tying it, all with the two ends fastened off, i.e. in the bight.

Method A

1 Form three identical closed loops with the centre loop bigger than the others.

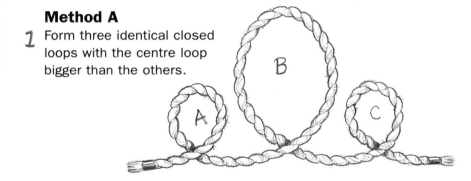

2 Take the left side of loop B over and through loop A. Then take the right side of loop B under and up through loop C.

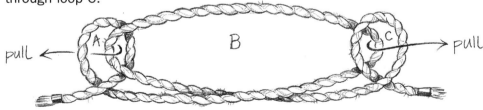

continued...

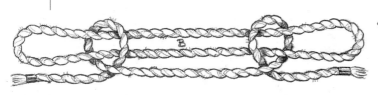

3 Adjust loop B so that it takes up the required amount of slack. The outer loop tightens round the inner loop to hold the hitch in place.

4 To secure the hitch in windy conditions, take the working parts through each loop and secure with pieces of wood.

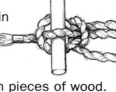

Method B

1 Form an 'S' shape in the slack of the rope. Form an underhand loop at the bottom end of the 'S'.

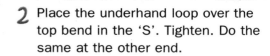

2 Place the underhand loop over the top bend in the 'S'. Tighten. Do the same at the other end.

3 Adjust the centre loop so that it takes up the required amount of slack.

Method C

1 Form an 'S' shape in the slack of the rope.

2 Take the top bight out and make a hitch around the lower single cord.

3 Pull firmly on the bight or loop end and transfer the hitch to the single cord. Repeat with the other bight.

pull

4 Adjust the centre loop so that it takes up the required amount of slack.

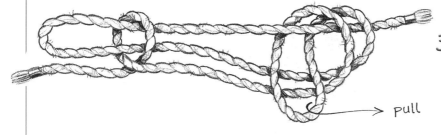

Marline Spike Hitch

This is a useful hitch which is tied in the bight and has the advantage of being easy to release. This hitch can also be used in pioneering, e.g. to fix and adjust rungs to a rope ladder.

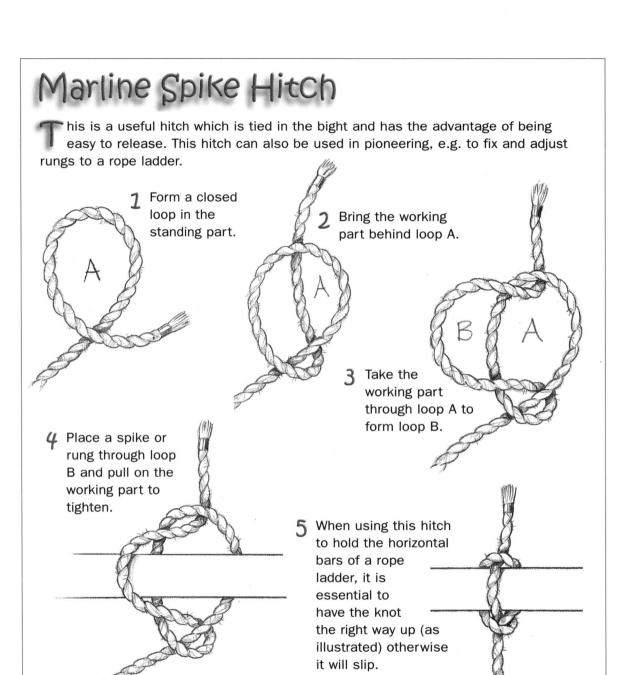

1 Form a closed loop in the standing part.

2 Bring the working part behind loop A.

3 Take the working part through loop A to form loop B.

4 Place a spike or rung through loop B and pull on the working part to tighten.

5 When using this hitch to hold the horizontal bars of a rope ladder, it is essential to have the knot the right way up (as illustrated) otherwise it will slip.

Bends

Sheet Bend

The Sheet Bend is probably the most familiar bend. It can be used to join cords of unequal thickness as long as the difference is not too great. It can also be used to join a cord to an Eye Splice (see page 90).

1 Form a bight in the thicker of the two cords to form an open loop. Take the working end of the thinner cord and pass it up through the loop.

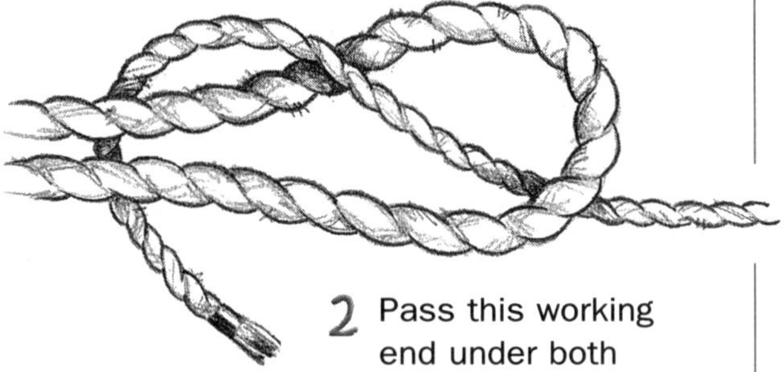

2 Pass this working end under both ends of the thicker cord.

3 Take the working end back across the first side of the loop and tuck it underneath itself.

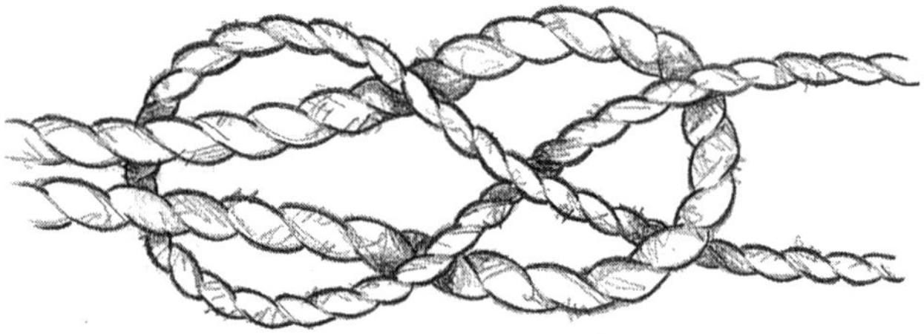

4 Pull all four ends to tighten the bend.

pull

pull

Pull

Pull

Fisherman's Knot

This is a joining knot for cords of even thickness and is particularly useful as it will slide apart fairly easily when the cords are wet. Should the cords be very stiff, however, the Fisherman's Knot may work loose, in which case the Double Fisherman's Knot (see page 50) would work better.

1 Place two cords parallel, the working ends in opposite directions.

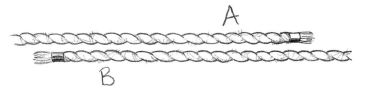

2 With the working end of cord A, tie a Thumb Knot (see page 10) around cord B.

3 With the working end of cord B, tie a Thumb Knot around cord A.

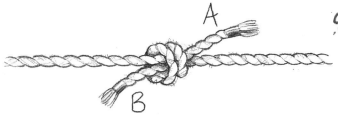

4 Pull both standing parts to slide the knots together. Work the knots so they fit snugly.

Double Fisherman's Knot

U sed in the same way and for the same purpose as the Fisherman's Knot, the extra twist gives some additional security when used in a fine, or smooth cord.

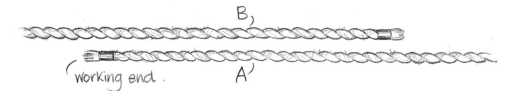

1 Place two cords parallel, the working ends in opposite directions as in the Fisherman's Knot (see page 49).

2 Take the working end of cord A over and round cord B and then behind itself.

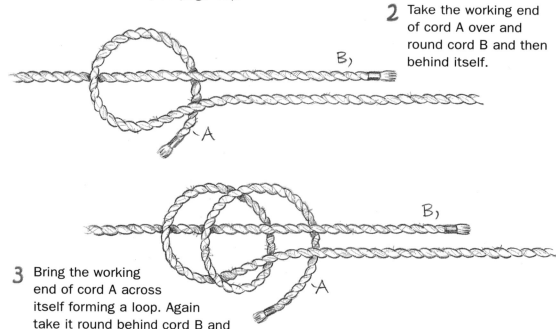

3 Bring the working end of cord A across itself forming a loop. Again take it round behind cord B and then behind itself.

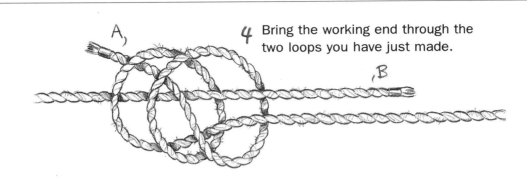

4 Bring the working end through the two loops you have just made.

5 Pull on the working end of cord A to tighten the knot.

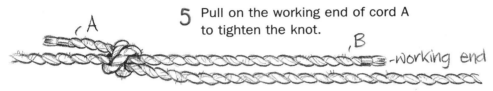

-working end

6 Repeat using cord B as the working end, tying the knot around cord A and finishing with the working ends lying parallel to the standing parts.

7 Pull both standing parts to slide the knots together. Work the knots so they fit snugly.

PULL ←   → PULL

Sliding Figure-of-Eight Knot

This knot has the same uses as the Fisherman's and Double Fisherman's Knots (see pages 49–51) but is more secure than the Fisherman's and less likely to jam than either of them.

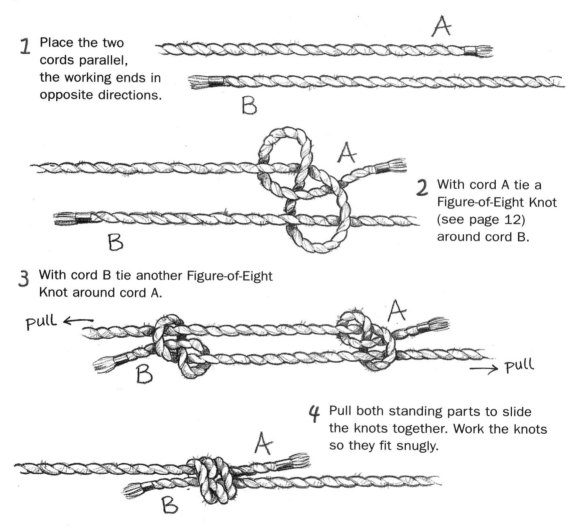

1 Place the two cords parallel, the working ends in opposite directions.

2 With cord A tie a Figure-of-Eight Knot (see page 12) around cord B.

3 With cord B tie another Figure-of-Eight Knot around cord A.

4 Pull both standing parts to slide the knots together. Work the knots so they fit snugly.

Carrick Bend

The Carrick Bend is a very old joining knot which, though less popular nowadays, is very secure when tied in thicker cords. Since it is also an attractive knot, it may be more familiar as a decorative knot and can be seen on many stone carvings.

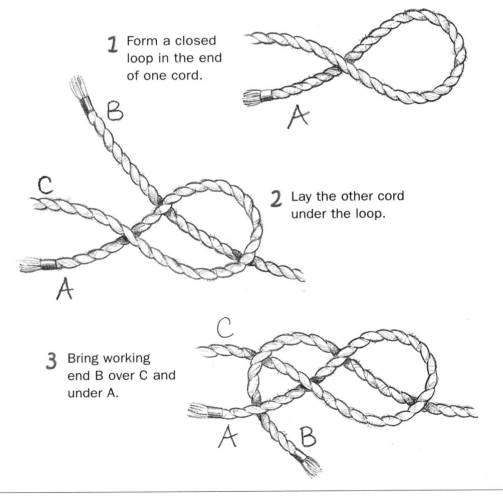

1 Form a closed loop in the end of one cord.

2 Lay the other cord under the loop.

3 Bring working end B over C and under A.

continued...

4 Then take working
end B over C, under
D and up through
the loop.

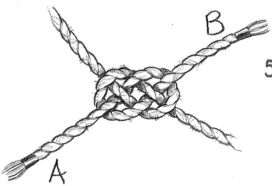

5 Gently pull the four ends to tighten
the knot. The knot should be flat
and with pressure on all four ends
will remain so. With pressure on
two opposing ends it will close up
into a secure joining knot.

Decorative Knotting

Lark's Head

The Lark's Head is used to attach a cord to a ring or bar as in macramé.

1 Double the cord to form an open loop and place a ring or other object on top of the loop.

2 Bring the closed end of the loop forward.

3 Pass the two ends of the cords through the loop and pull to tighten.

Square Knot (English) or Friendship Knot

This knot is used to tie a scarf or neckerchief.

1 Form two open loops in the standing end of the cord.

2 Take the working end up through loop A and over the cords of loop B.

3 Bring the working end behind the two loops.

continued...

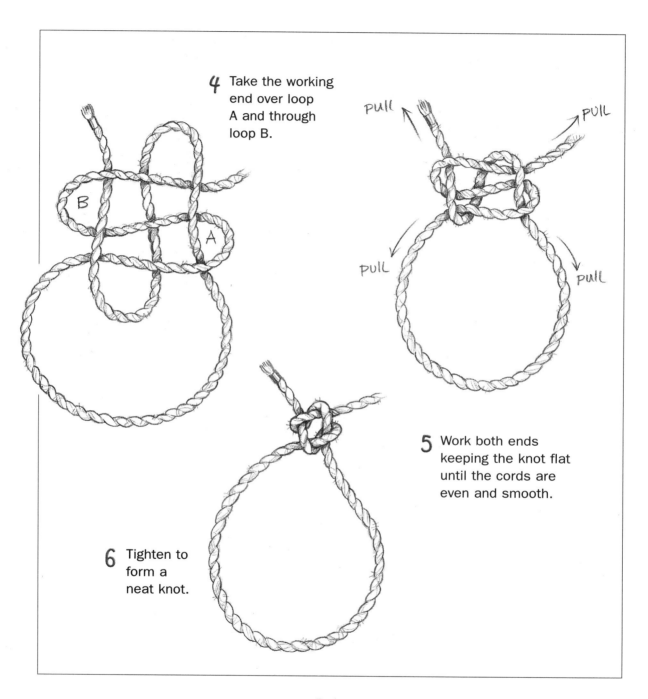

4 Take the working end over loop A and through loop B.

PULL
PULL
PULL
PULL

5 Work both ends keeping the knot flat until the cords are even and smooth.

6 Tighten to form a neat knot.

True Lover's Knot

The True Lover's Knot is very decorative. Look out for it on jewellery – especially rings. It can be tied using one or two cords. We have tied it with just one cord in this example.

2 Bring the working end over the standing part and pass it under to form an Underhand Knot.

1 Form an open loop in one end of the cord.

3 Take the standing end and bring it over the loop in the first knot and then back under.

4 Pass the standing end under itself and through to form an Overhand Knot.

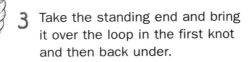

5 Tighten the knot so that the two parts lock together.

Shamrock Knot

This knot can be tied from a True Lover's Knot (see page 59) and is not as complicated as it looks. It is attractive in cord, ribbon and on jewellery.

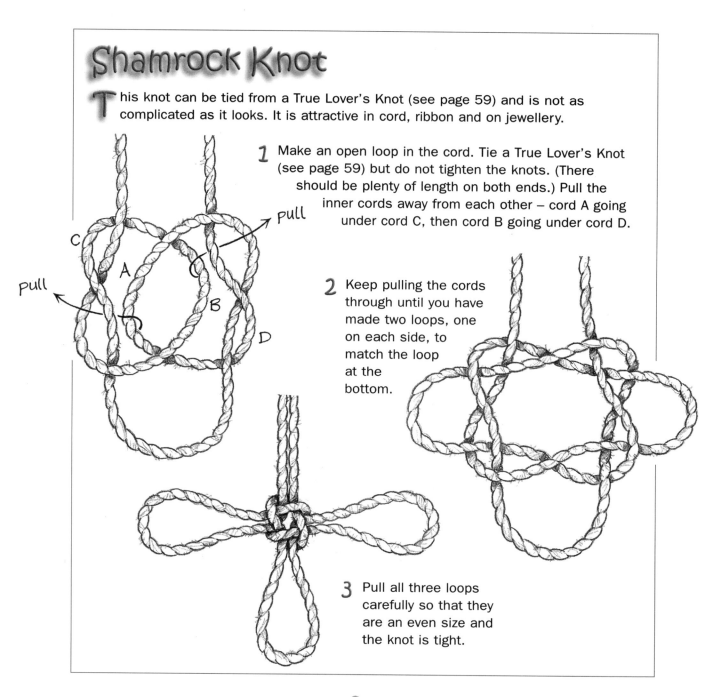

1 Make an open loop in the cord. Tie a True Lover's Knot (see page 59) but do not tighten the knots. (There should be plenty of length on both ends.) Pull the inner cords away from each other – cord A going under cord C, then cord B going under cord D.

2 Keep pulling the cords through until you have made two loops, one on each side, to match the loop at the bottom.

3 Pull all three loops carefully so that they are an even size and the knot is tight.

Turk's Head

The Turk's Head is often used as a decorative knot and is ideal for making woggles, but it can be very practical, too, as it is technically a binding knot. Once you have mastered the basic knot you can develop it into more complex patterns.

1 Form a Clove Hitch (see page 37) around a pole. Remove working end A from the hitch.

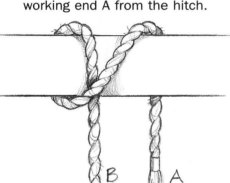

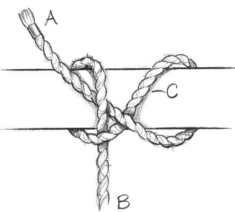

2 Lay working end A over C and pass it under B.

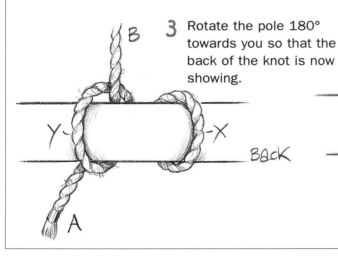

3 Rotate the pole 180° towards you so that the back of the knot is now showing.

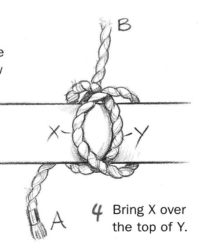

4 Bring X over the top of Y.

continued...

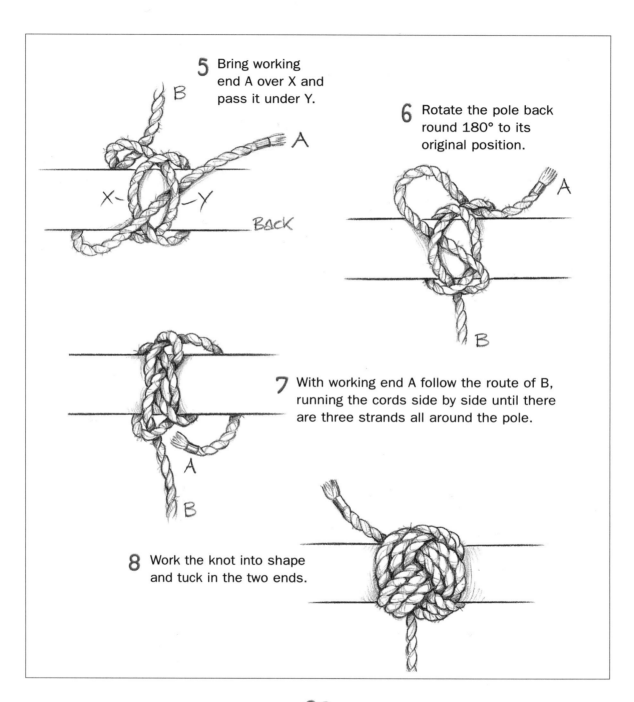

5 Bring working end A over X and pass it under Y.

B

A

X

Y

BACK

6 Rotate the pole back round 180° to its original position.

A

B

7 With working end A follow the route of B, running the cords side by side until there are three strands all around the pole.

A

B

8 Work the knot into shape and tuck in the two ends.

Boatswain's Weave or Flat Portuguese Sennit

A flat plait which is very decorative, especially if you use two colours of cord – one colour for the core cords and one for the working ends.

1 Secure the four cords – two for the central core and two working ends. Bring end A over the core (inner) cords and pass it under end B. This will form loop C.

2 Bring end B under the core cords and up through loop C. Pull the knot tight.

3 Take end A over the core. Then take end B over A, behind the core and up through loop D. Pull the knot tight.

4 Repeat Steps 1, 2 and 3 for a long weave.

Rolling Boatswain

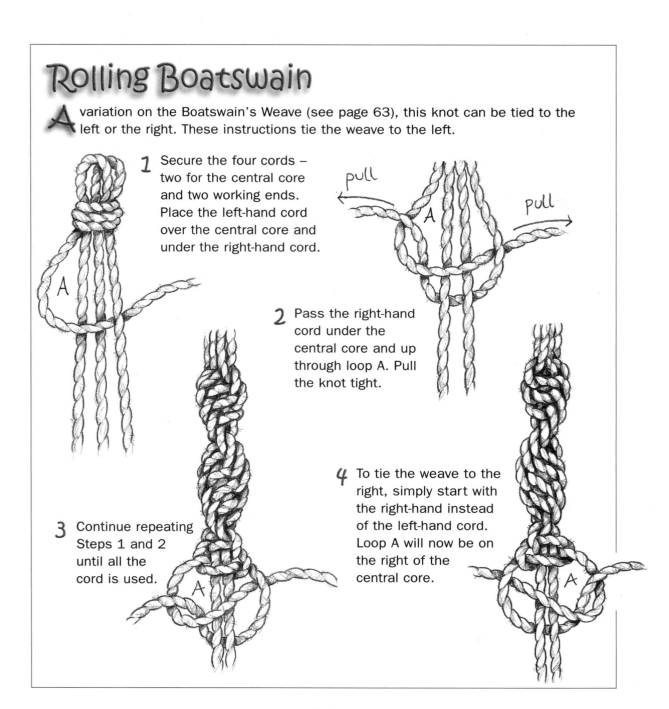

A variation on the Boatswain's Weave (see page 63), this knot can be tied to the left or the right. These instructions tie the weave to the left.

1 Secure the four cords – two for the central core and two working ends. Place the left-hand cord over the central core and under the right-hand cord.

pull

pull

2 Pass the right-hand cord under the central core and up through loop A. Pull the knot tight.

3 Continue repeating Steps 1 and 2 until all the cord is used.

4 To tie the weave to the right, simply start with the right-hand instead of the left-hand cord. Loop A will now be on the right of the central core.

Grapevine or Corkscrew Bar

This knot is attractive and also useful, as it is good for using surplus ends. The knots are tied around a central core which can be formed of any number of cords. Four cords are used to tie this Grapevine.

1 Secure the four cords – three for the core and one working end. Take one of the outside cords (this will be the working end) and pass it round behind the central core. Tie a Half Hitch (see page 24) and pull tight. Bring the hitch to the top of the cords.

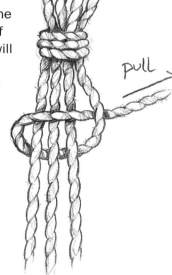

pull →

2 Repeat Step 1 always using the same working end and keeping the Half Hitches tight and close together.

3 Continue until a spiral is formed.

See-Saw Knot

The See-Saw Knot consists of alternate Half Hitches (see page 24). It is probably more effective and decorative if it is tied in doubled cords.

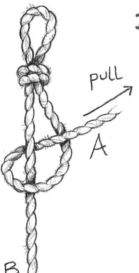

1 Secure the cord so there are two working ends. With cord A tie a Half Hitch (see page 24) around cord B and pull to the top.

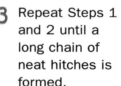

2 With cord B, tie a Half Hitch around cord A and work up to the first Half Hitch.

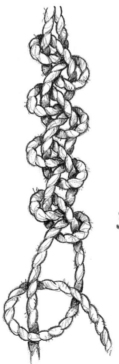

3 Repeat Steps 1 and 2 until a long chain of neat hitches is formed.

Half-Hitch Lanterns

This open work is based on the See-Saw Knot (see page 66). Eight lengths of cord are used. This example has been tied to a ring so it is clearer to see from the drawings how this knot is formed. If tying this knot as part of a lanyard or friendship bracelet you will not need to use a ring and can therefore skip Step 1 and simply start with eight lengths of cord.

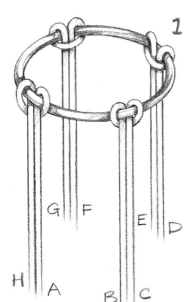

1 Take four cords and double them. Form a Lark's Head (see page 56) over a ring with each doubled cord so that the cords are of even length. Space out the Lark's Heads so that they are an equal distance apart.

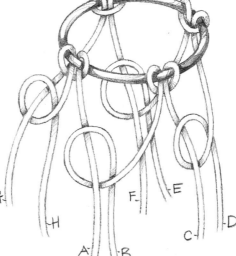

2 Pair off each cord by taking those next to each other, these pairs will be A + B, C + D, E + F, G + H.

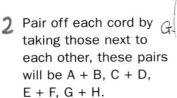

continued...

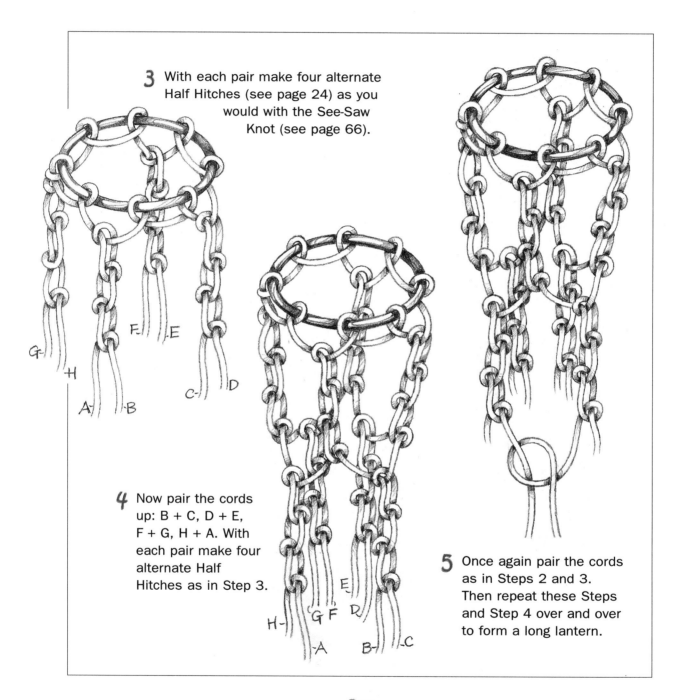

3 With each pair make four alternate Half Hitches (see page 24) as you would with the See-Saw Knot (see page 66).

G-

H

A-   -B

F-   -E

C-   -D

4 Now pair the cords up: B + C, D + E, F + G, H + A. With each pair make four alternate Half Hitches as in Step 3.

H-   -A

G F   E

D-   B-   -C

5 Once again pair the cords as in Steps 2 and 3. Then repeat these Steps and Step 4 over and over to form a long lantern.

Flat Sennit

The Flat Sennit is tied using five cords. The outer cords are moved alternately to form an attractive plait.

1 Secure the cords so there are five working ends. Pass the outside right-hand cord over the two cords next to it and into the centre.

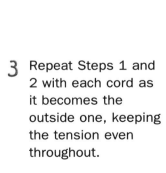

2 Pass the outside left-hand cord over the two cords next to it (this will include the cord from Step 1).

3 Repeat Steps 1 and 2 with each cord as it becomes the outside one, keeping the tension even throughout.

North, South, East and West

A four-strand plait which gives a square formation when completed. Tie it using two doubled cords or four single.

1 Secure the cords so there are four working ends. Pass the outside right-hand cord behind the two next to it and then back over the second cord.

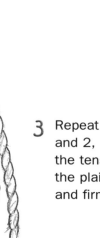

2 Pass the outside left-hand cord behind the two cords that are now next to it and then back over the second one.

3 Repeat Steps 1 and 2, keeping the tension on the plait even and firm.

Dragonfly

This decorative knot is for the more experienced knotter and can be two or three cords in thickness. Tie it using a firm cord – approximately 1 to 1.5 metres of cord is needed. Why not turn it into a pretty badge by adding some feathers and a safety pin?

1 Divide the cord in half and pass it around a pole. Tie a Turk's Head (see pages 61–62) in the centre of the cord. Work through with one end and then in the reverse direction with the other end. This will keep the cords even in length. Let the Turk's Head close up to make a round ball with two long cords. This gives the Dragonfly's head.

2 Tie a True Lover's Knot (see page 59) using the two long cords.

3 Tie a Shamrock Knot (see page 60) with the Turk's Head as the third leaf of the Shamrock to form the Dragonfly's wings. Tie another Shamrock Knot to make the second set of wings. Leave the two ends loose to form a tail.

Round Crowning or Spiral Plait

This makes a thick round plait very firm and attractive. It can be used for the centre front of a lanyard, a bell rope or pull cord. Crowning can be tied around a central core or with just the cords. This Round Crowning is tied using four cords. At first it may be easier to work with four different coloured cords.

1 Secure the cords and hold them in your hand so that you are looking into the centre of the plait. Work towards yourself.

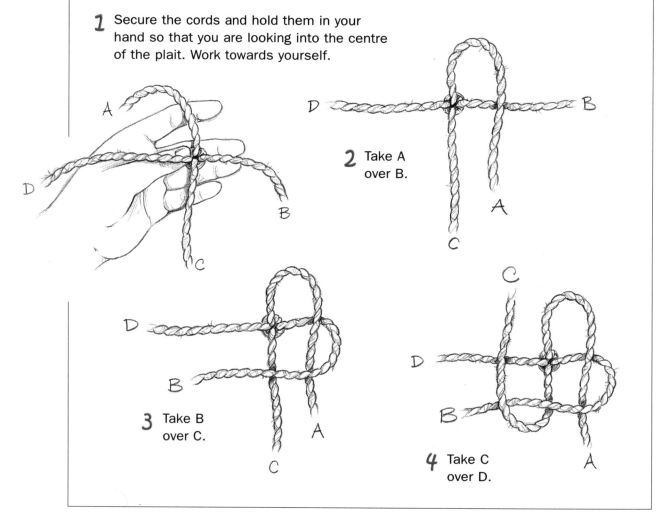

2 Take A over B.

3 Take B over C.

4 Take C over D.

72

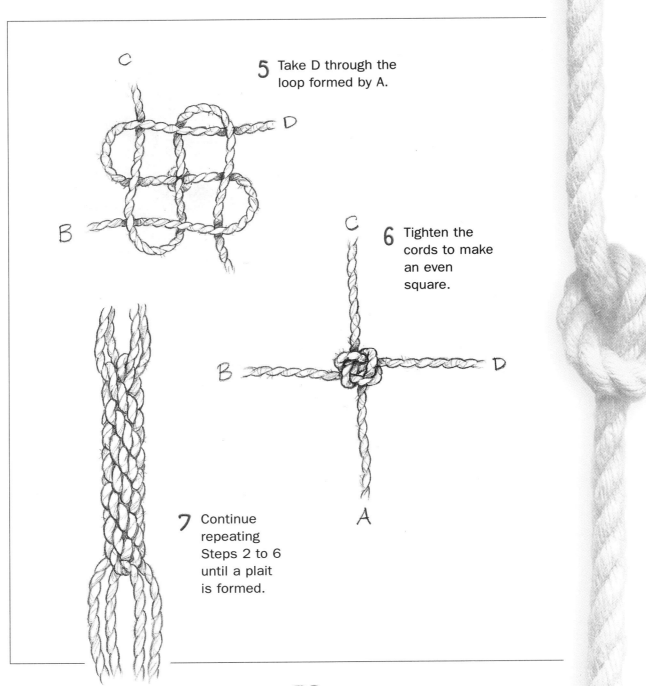

5 Take D through the loop formed by A.

6 Tighten the cords to make an even square.

7 Continue repeating Steps 2 to 6 until a plait is formed.

Square Crowning

Similar to Round Crowning but the alternate rounds are reversed. The first round is plaited clockwise, the second round is plaited anti-clockwise. Make sure a round is fully completed before changing direction. Start by using four different coloured cords, then experiment by using single cords around a central core or doubled cords.

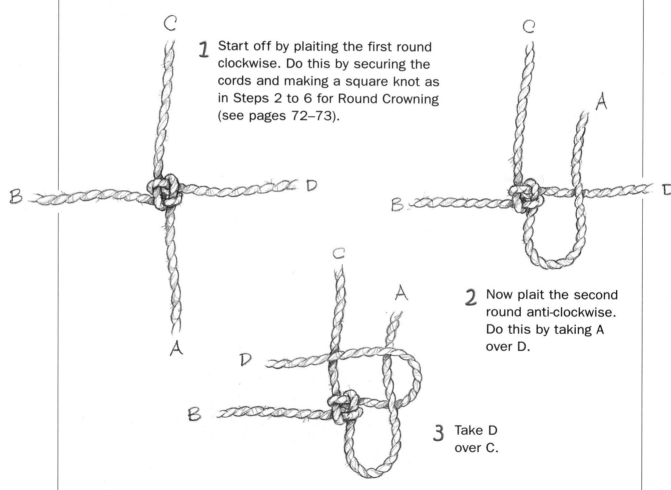

1 Start off by plaiting the first round clockwise. Do this by securing the cords and making a square knot as in Steps 2 to 6 for Round Crowning (see pages 72–73).

2 Now plait the second round anti-clockwise. Do this by taking A over D.

3 Take D over C.

4 Take C over B.

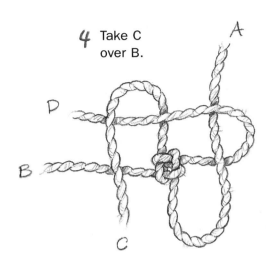

5 Take B through the loop formed by A. Tighten the square.

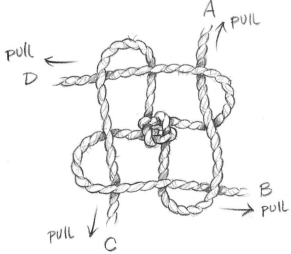

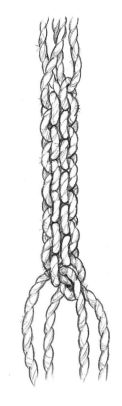

6 Continue plaiting alternate rounds – clockwise and anti-clockwise – by repeating Steps 2 to 5 until a plait is formed.

Chain Sennit or Simple Plait

This is exactly like chain stitch in crocheting but using your fingers rather than a hook! It is useful for shortening a long rope – especially if it is to be carried – or as an alternative to coiling or looping a nylon or plastic rope, e.g. the type used for making rafts.

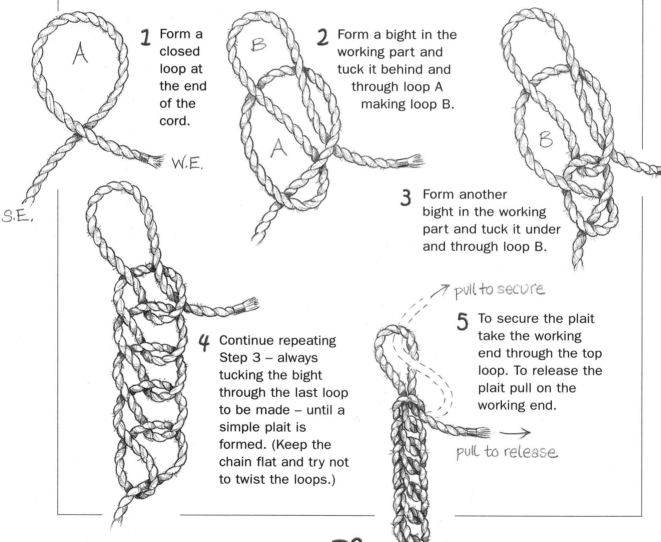

1 Form a closed loop at the end of the cord.

2 Form a bight in the working part and tuck it behind and through loop A making loop B.

3 Form another bight in the working part and tuck it under and through loop B.

4 Continue repeating Step 3 – always tucking the bight through the last loop to be made – until a simple plait is formed. (Keep the chain flat and try not to twist the loops.)

5 To secure the plait take the working end through the top loop. To release the plait pull on the working end.

pull to secure

pull to release

76

Lanyard Making

Lanyards are knotted cords to which a knife or whistle may be attached. For a long time, making a lanyard was part of the tradition of the Senior Section members. Many people now use the same knots for friendship bracelets to exchange with new friends – or to sell! For details on making friendship bracelets see *A World of Ideas*.

When making a lanyard there is a tendency to tie the knots and plaits too loosely – they need to be firm and the whole of any one phase even. To make this lanyard you will need 2 x 15 m lengths of Plaiter's Line (a very fine cotton cord – if you use nylon it may not sit together so well).

1 Cut each hank in half and tie the four lengths together about one third of the way down. Tie the top third together – folding and securing with an Overhand Knot (page 10) or a Slip Knot (page 21) – to keep it out of the way. The four long ends (two thirds of the length) will be the working ends. Wind each one around a short length of card to avoid them getting muddled.

continued...

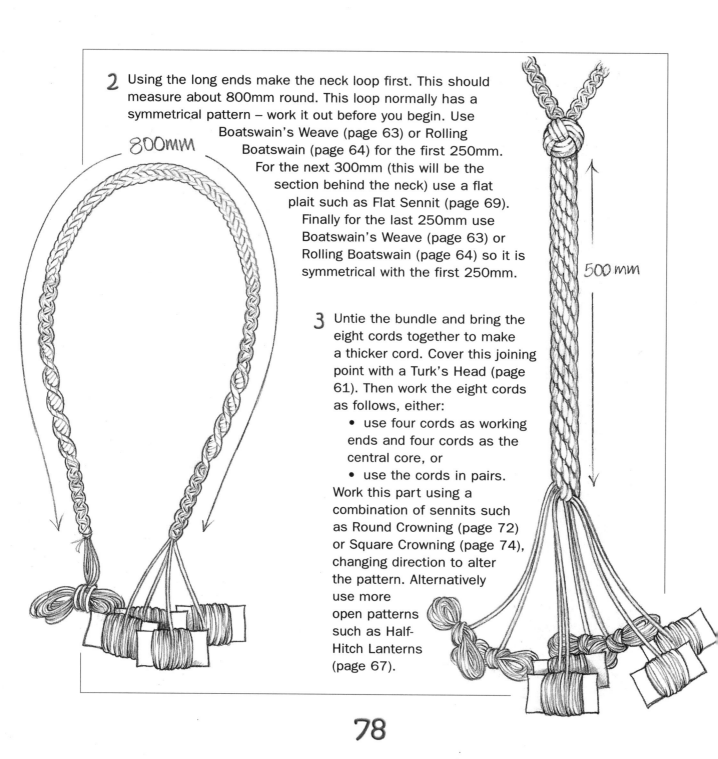

2 Using the long ends make the neck loop first. This should measure about 800mm round. This loop normally has a symmetrical pattern – work it out before you begin. Use Boatswain's Weave (page 63) or Rolling Boatswain (page 64) for the first 250mm. For the next 300mm (this will be the section behind the neck) use a flat plait such as Flat Sennit (page 69). Finally for the last 250mm use Boatswain's Weave (page 63) or Rolling Boatswain (page 64) so it is symmetrical with the first 250mm.

3 Untie the bundle and bring the eight cords together to make a thicker cord. Cover this joining point with a Turk's Head (page 61). Then work the eight cords as follows, either:

• use four cords as working ends and four cords as the central core, or

• use the cords in pairs.

Work this part using a combination of sennits such as Round Crowning (page 72) or Square Crowning (page 74), changing direction to alter the pattern. Alternatively use more open patterns such as Half-Hitch Lanterns (page 67).

800MM

500 mm

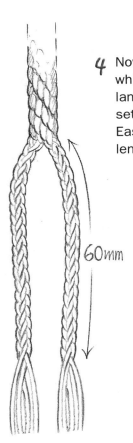

4 Now you need to make the end loop which attaches a knife or whistle to the lanyard. Divide the main cord into two sets of four cords. Use North, South, East and West (page 70) to make two lengths about 60mm long.

60mm

5 Bring the two lengths together using Square Crowning (page 74) for about 10mm. Finish this part with a Turk's Head (page 61). Knot each end with a Figure-of-Eight Knot (page 12) and fringe the ends. Alternatively thread the ends back up through the short-end section.

Tricks

Lots & Lots of Thumb Knots

This is sometimes known as the Magical Knot, the Fireman's Knot or the Philadelphia Knot.

1 Tie four Half Hitches (see page 24) in a row around your thumb making sure the working end finishes at the top of your thumb. Leave the hitches fairly loose.

2 Take the working end down through the hitches. Pulling it gently through.

3 Slide the hitches off your thumb and continue to pull the working end through. Hey presto you are left with a row of thumb knots!

The Disappearing Knot

Now you see it, now you don't! Amaze your friends with this trick. Once you have mastered the Thumb Knot (see page 10) this trick should be easy to do. Try it using a really firm cord.

1 Perform Lots and Lots of Thumb Knots (see page 10) but keep the knots very loosely tied. Put the Thumb Knots (in the order they came off your thumb) into the palm of your hand. At the same time tuck the working end back through the loop of each Thumb Knot. Hold the standing end between your first and second finger and the working end between your little and ring finger.

W.E.

pull

pull

W.E

pull

2 Close up your hand to form a fist. Ask two members of your audience to pull on the two ends, telling them that by doing this the knots will be tied as tight as possible and so difficult to untie.

3 When they have finished, pull on the working end to check if it is really tight. The cord will magically pull through without a knot to be seen.

Lots of Figure-of-Eight Knots

This is similar to the Lots and Lots of Thumb Knots trick but by putting an extra twist in the cord each time, you will end up with a row of Figure-of-Eight Knots.

1 Form a closed loop. Twist the loop 180° in a clockwise direction.

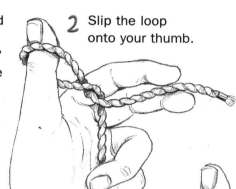

2 Slip the loop onto your thumb.

3 Take your working end and form another loop as in Step 1 and slip onto your thumb. Repeat this three or four times.

4 Take the working end and thread it down through the loops – sliding them off your thumb one by one as the cord passes through.

5 Carefully continue to work the cord through until you have a row of three or four Figure-of-Eight Knots.

Removing a Cord from a Ring

You can do this trick through a ring, a key or a buttonhole – practise before trying it on someone else's buttonhole! Make sure you follow the diagrams carefully otherwise the trick will not work.

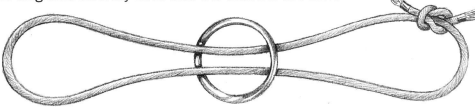

1 Run the doubled cord smoothly through the ring.

2 Slip each end over each of your thumbs making sure you keep the cord straight. Do not let it cross.

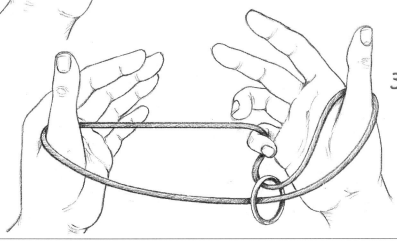

3 Keeping the cord firm pick up a loop in the cord using first the little finger on your right hand and then the little finger on your left.

continued...

4 Make sure your cord looks exactly as in the picture
(below). Then slip the cord off the little finger on
your left hand and the thumb on your right hand at
the same time.

5 Pull your hands apart to
straighten the cord and the
ring will drop free.

Cutting Fingers

There are several ways of 'cutting fingers' with a cord. Try this one first, then look up some other ways of performing this trick.

1 Knot the cord to form a complete circle.

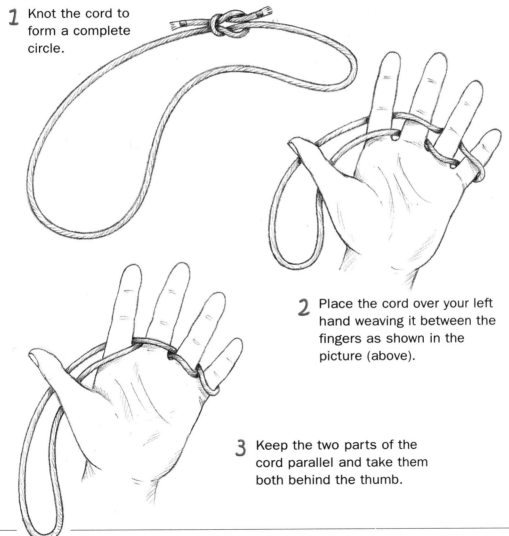

2 Place the cord over your left hand weaving it between the fingers as shown in the picture (above).

3 Keep the two parts of the cord parallel and take them both behind the thumb.

continued...

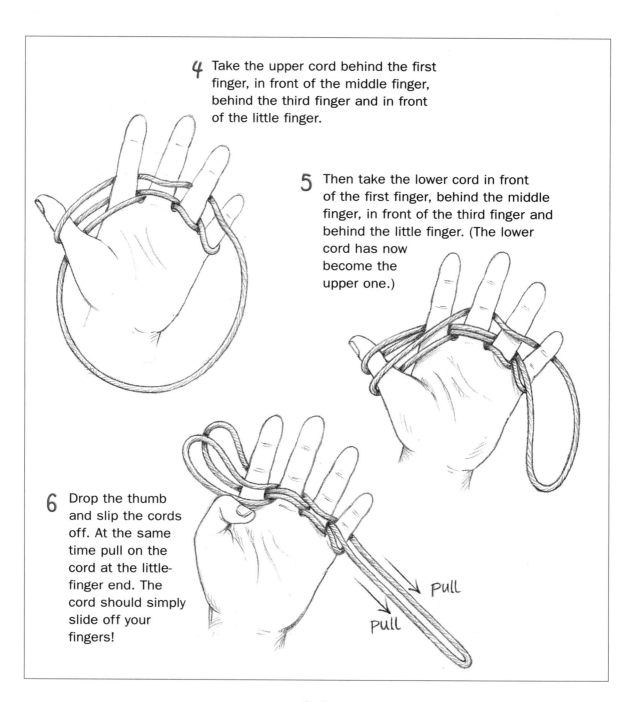

4 Take the upper cord behind the first finger, in front of the middle finger, behind the third finger and in front of the little finger.

5 Then take the lower cord in front of the first finger, behind the middle finger, in front of the third finger and behind the little finger. (The lower cord has now become the upper one.)

6 Drop the thumb and slip the cords off. At the same time pull on the cord at the little-finger end. The cord should simply slide off your fingers!

Pull

Pull

Splices

Eye Splice

The Eye Splice makes a secure and permanent loop in the end of a rope.

1 Undo the strands at one end of the rope. Secure with a piece of string to stop the strands unravelling further.

2 Lay the three strands across the standing part so you have a loop that is the size you require. Twist the standing part to open the strands at the point you want to start the splice. Thread the middle strand A under the open strand.

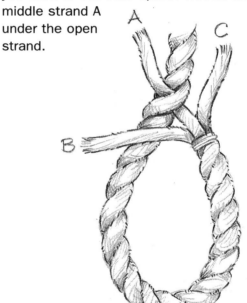

3 Twist the rope again to open the strands. Thread strand B over one strand and under the next.

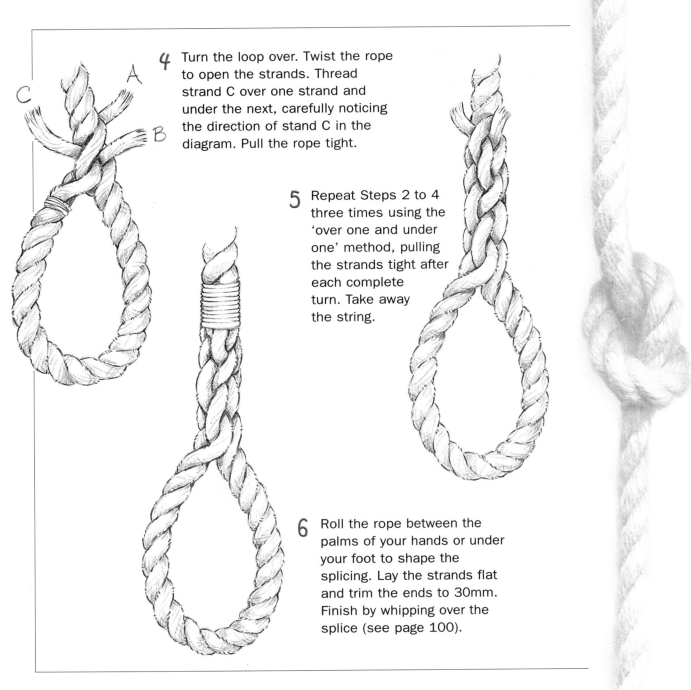

4 Turn the loop over. Twist the rope to open the strands. Thread strand C over one strand and under the next, carefully noticing the direction of stand C in the diagram. Pull the rope tight.

5 Repeat Steps 2 to 4 three times using the 'over one and under one' method, pulling the strands tight after each complete turn. Take away the string.

6 Roll the rope between the palms of your hands or under your foot to shape the splicing. Lay the strands flat and trim the ends to 30mm. Finish by whipping over the splice (see page 100).

C   A

B

Crown Knot

This knot prevents a rope unravelling and also starts a Back Splice (see page 93).

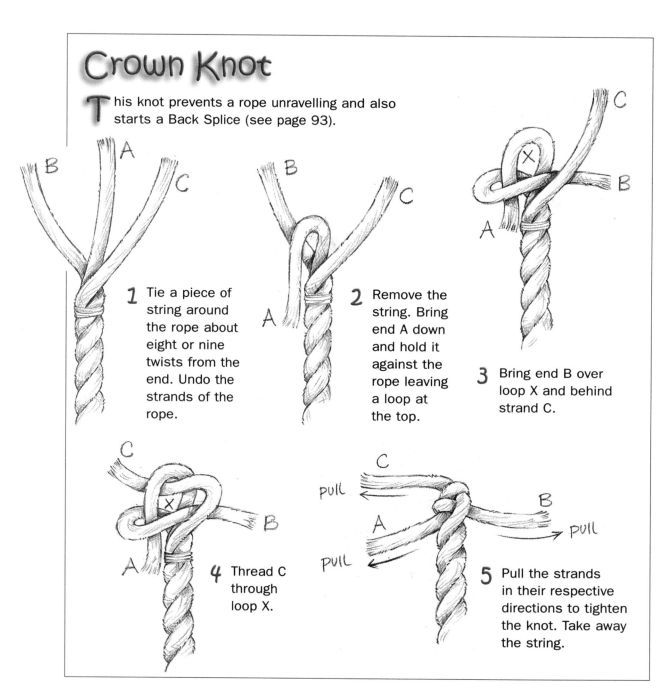

1 Tie a piece of string around the rope about eight or nine twists from the end. Undo the strands of the rope.

2 Remove the string. Bring end A down and hold it against the rope leaving a loop at the top.

3 Bring end B over loop X and behind strand C.

4 Thread C through loop X.

5 Pull the strands in their respective directions to tighten the knot. Take away the string.

Back Splice

This is the best way to stop the end of a rope unravelling. It can be used as an alternative to whipping.

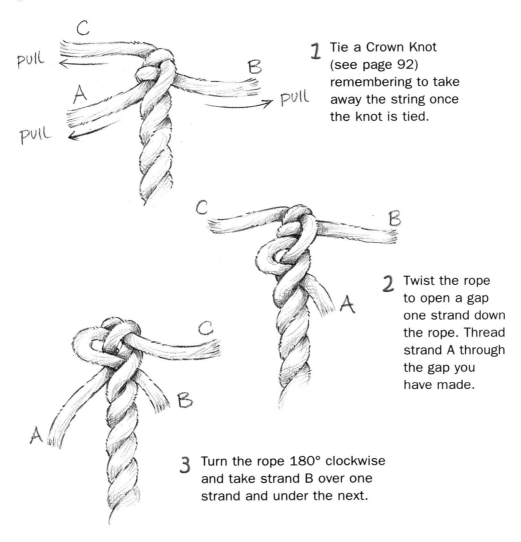

1 Tie a Crown Knot (see page 92) remembering to take away the string once the knot is tied.

2 Twist the rope to open a gap one strand down the rope. Thread strand A through the gap you have made.

3 Turn the rope 180° clockwise and take strand B over one strand and under the next.

continued...

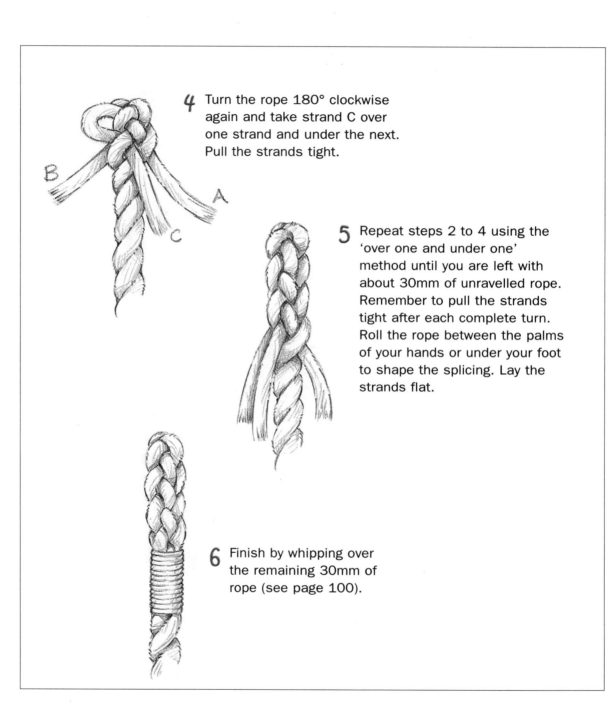

4 Turn the rope 180° clockwise again and take strand C over one strand and under the next. Pull the strands tight.

5 Repeat steps 2 to 4 using the 'over one and under one' method until you are left with about 30mm of unravelled rope. Remember to pull the strands tight after each complete turn. Roll the rope between the palms of your hands or under your foot to shape the splicing. Lay the strands flat.

6 Finish by whipping over the remaining 30mm of rope (see page 100).

Short Splice

The Short Splice is the most efficient method of joining two ropes of equal thickness. However it cannot be used if the rope has to pass through the eye of a block, because it will be too thick.

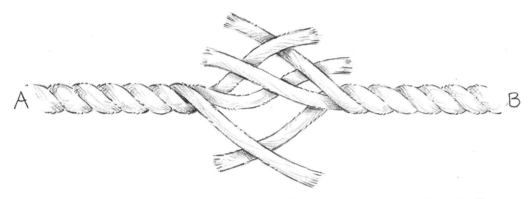

1 Take two ropes and undo the strands of each to the required length. Then interlock the strands so they go alternately between the strands of the other rope.

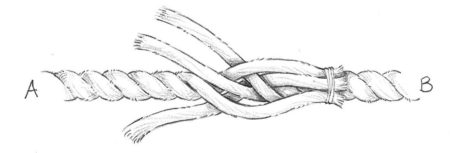

2 Push the ropes together. Run the strands from rope A down to rope B and tie some string around the strands to keep them out the way. Make sure these strands are kept tight. Now you are ready to start splicing.

continued...

3 Splice the strands from rope B onto rope A, turning clockwise and using the 'over one and under one' method as for the Back Splice (see page 93). Do this five times, remembering to tighten the strands after each turn.

4 When you have completed five turns, roll the rope between the palms of your hands or under your foot to shape the splicing and lay the strands flat. Trim the ends to 30mm. Finish by whipping over the end of the rope (see page 100).

5 Untie the strands of rope A and you are ready to splice rope A onto rope B. To do this repeat Steps 3 and 4 above.

Long Splice

This is the only splice which will run through a block and is used for replacing a halyard on a flagpole.

1 Undo the strands of the ropes by 300mm. Interlock the strands as the Short Splice (see page 95).

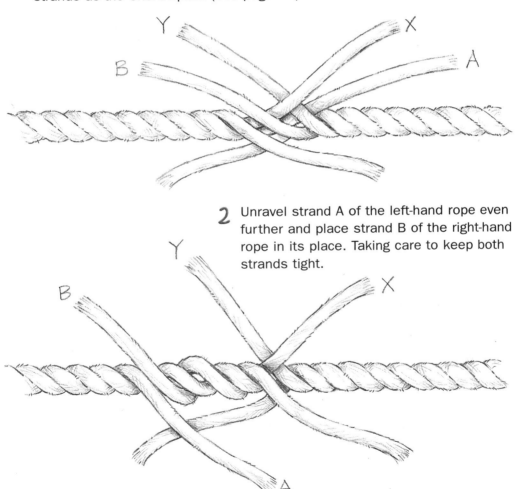

2 Unravel strand A of the left-hand rope even further and place strand B of the right-hand rope in its place. Taking care to keep both strands tight.

continued...

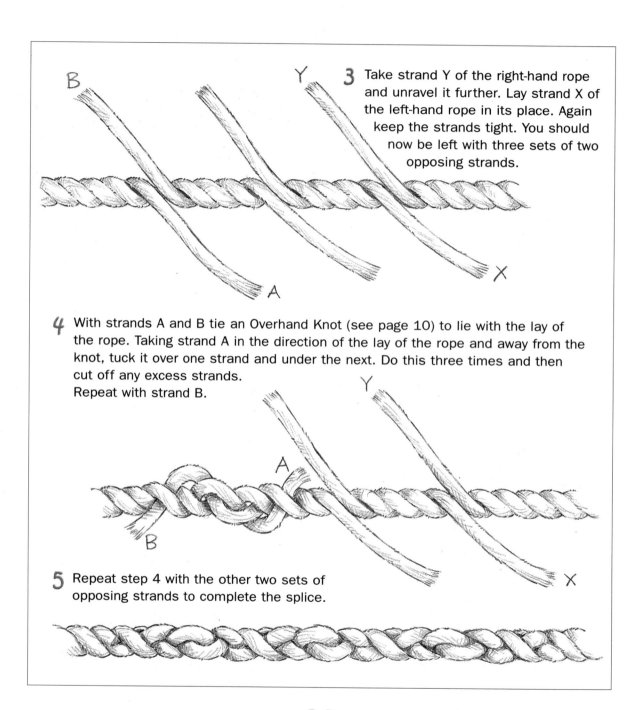

3 Take strand Y of the right-hand rope and unravel it further. Lay strand X of the left-hand rope in its place. Again keep the strands tight. You should now be left with three sets of two opposing strands.

4 With strands A and B tie an Overhand Knot (see page 10) to lie with the lay of the rope. Taking strand A in the direction of the lay of the rope and away from the knot, tuck it over one strand and under the next. Do this three times and then cut off any excess strands.
Repeat with strand B.

5 Repeat step 4 with the other two sets of opposing strands to complete the splice.

Whippings

Simple Whipping

Rope made from natural fibres such as hemp, sisal, flax and cotton can be whipped using fine but strong twine to bind the end and stop it fraying. The length of the whipping should be about the same as the diameter of the rope to be whipped.

1 Form an open loop in the twine and lay it parallel to the rope.

2 Wind the working end of the twine around the rope and loop, working your way towards the rope end. Pull the twine as tight as you can keeping the turns side by side – work to about 50mm from the end of the rope.

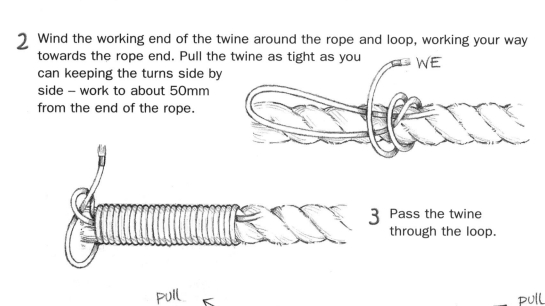

3 Pass the twine through the loop.

4 Pull on the standing end until the loop is about half way down the whipping. Trim the ends.

Sailmaker's Whipping

This whipping is very strong and durable because the twine is interwoven between the strands of the rope.

1 Untie the strands of the rope by about 70mm. Make an open loop in the end of the twine and lay it loosely over strand X. Bring the working end and the standing end out between the other two strands.

working end

2 Leave the open loop loose and wind the working end firmly around the rope until the desired length has been completed.

3 Hold the working end tight against the rope and take the loop over the top of strand X. Pull the standing end tight.

pull

4 Pull the standing end up to the end of the rope to form a third diagonal across the whipping. Finish by tying a Reef Knot (see page 14) which lies hidden in the centre of the strands.

West Country Whipping

This decorative whipping can be used not only to prevent a rope from fraying, but also as an alternative to Sheer-Leg Lashing (see page 111), e.g. to whip two poles together to make a flagpole. If it is being used to lash two poles together you may need thicker twine, two lengths of whipping and a wedge to secure the structure.

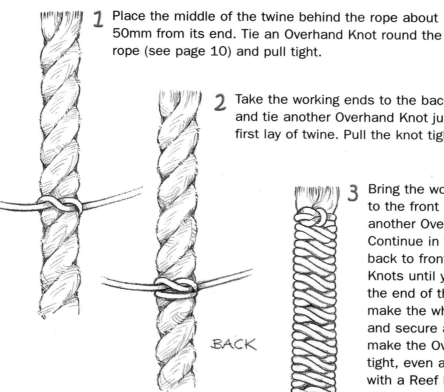

1 Place the middle of the twine behind the rope about 50mm from its end. Tie an Overhand Knot round the rope (see page 10) and pull tight.

2 Take the working ends to the back of the rope and tie another Overhand Knot just above the first lay of twine. Pull the knot tight.

BACK

3 Bring the working ends back to the front again and tie another Overhand Knot. Continue in this way from back to front tying Overhand Knots until you are nearly at the end of the rope. To make the whipping as neat and secure as possible, make the Overhand Knots tight, even and level. Finish with a Reef Knot (see page 14) and tuck in the ends.

Lashings

Introduction

Lashing is used to fix two or more poles together e.g. in structures such as bridges or scaffolding. The secret of good lashing is to make sure it is pulled tightly and securely with an even tension throughout. You must also make sure the lashing is laid neatly side by side around the poles – never overlapping.

In Guiding lashings are used in water activities, such as raft-making, but more commonly they are used in the making of gadgets for camp, and in a variety of pioneering projects.

You can use various materials for lashing – anything from string to thick rope – depending on the use of your structure, e.g. if you are building a structure that will be bearing human weight such as a swing, a thicker rope needs to be used. Refer to the sections on Camp Gadgets (see page 114) and Pioneering (see page 120) for further information about materials. With confidence in the use of just a few lashings, it is possible for you to make a number of structures – safely and securely – and to use them.

Frapping

Frapping is a term used in lashing. Once you have lashed your poles together – taking the lashing around the wood – you will find that the structure has a tendency to wobble about. Your structure has to be secure so you must then take the cord around the lashing rather than around the wood. These are known as frapping turns and in each description of a lashing you will find reference to these. Remember the frapping turns are the ones that secure the initial part of the lashing, therefore make sure they are tight and are finished off securely.

Square Lashing

This lashing will join two poles together to form a secure cross. There are two possible methods.

Method A

1 Tie a Clove Hitch (see page 37) around the vertical pole leaving end B fairly short. Place the second pole horizontally above the Clove Hitch.

2 Take working end A over W, behind Z, over Y and behind X.

3 Repeat Step 2 four times pulling the cord tight after each turn.

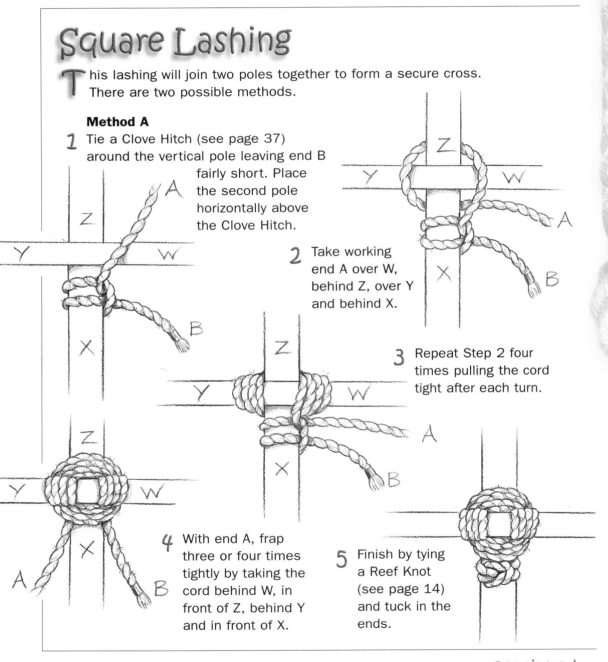

4 With end A, frap three or four times tightly by taking the cord behind W, in front of Z, behind Y and in front of X.

5 Finish by tying a Reef Knot (see page 14) and tuck in the ends.

continued...

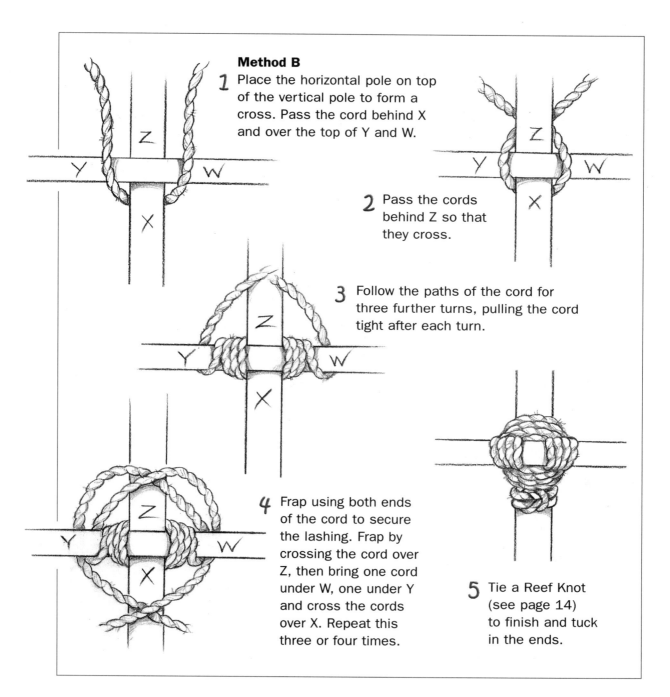

Method B

1 Place the horizontal pole on top of the vertical pole to form a cross. Pass the cord behind X and over the top of Y and W.

2 Pass the cords behind Z so that they cross.

3 Follow the paths of the cord for three further turns, pulling the cord tight after each turn.

4 Frap using both ends of the cord to secure the lashing. Frap by crossing the cord over Z, then bring one cord under W, one under Y and cross the cords over X. Repeat this three or four times.

5 Tie a Reef Knot (see page 14) to finish and tuck in the ends.

106

Snake Lashing

This lashing is used to secure several short poles to a longer pole and is used to make a table-top or washing-up rack at camp.

1 Find the middle of the cord and tie a Clove Hitch (see page 37) around one end of a long pole.

2 Lay a short pole across the longer pole, below the hitch. Bring both ends over the short pole and cross the cords behind the long pole.

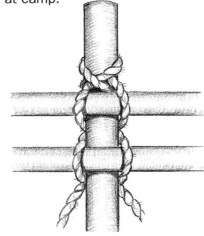

3 Lay another short pole below the first one and repeat Step 2 keeping the cords tight.

4 Continue until all the horizontal poles are in place.

5 Take the working cords around the longer pole and finish by tying the ends with a Reef Knot (see page 14).

To make a table-top, attach the other end of the short poles to a long pole in the same way.

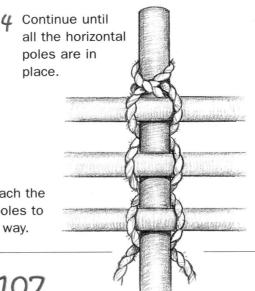

Tripod Lashing

ripod Lashing is used to secure three poles together to form a tripod. A tripod makes an excellent gadget for campers and is the basis of some of the structures in the pioneering projects (see page 120).

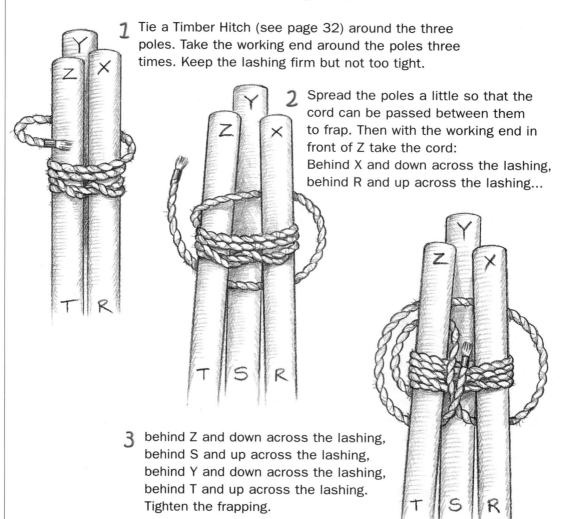

1 Tie a Timber Hitch (see page 32) around the three poles. Take the working end around the poles three times. Keep the lashing firm but not too tight.

2 Spread the poles a little so that the cord can be passed between them to frap. Then with the working end in front of Z take the cord:
Behind X and down across the lashing, behind R and up across the lashing...

3 behind Z and down across the lashing, behind S and up across the lashing, behind Y and down across the lashing, behind T and up across the lashing. Tighten the frapping.

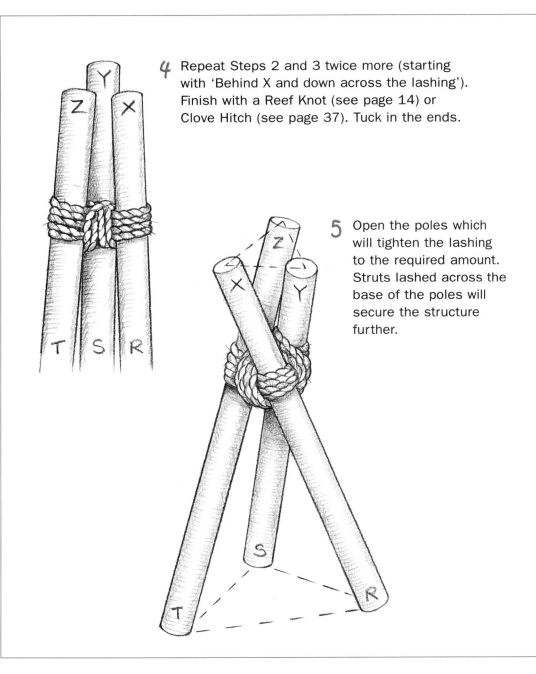

4 Repeat Steps 2 and 3 twice more (starting with 'Behind X and down across the lashing'). Finish with a Reef Knot (see page 14) or Clove Hitch (see page 37). Tuck in the ends.

5 Open the poles which will tighten the lashing to the required amount. Struts lashed across the base of the poles will secure the structure further.

Diagonal Lashing

U sed to secure two diagonal poles to stop them from springing apart, Diagonal Lashing is often the added extra which makes a gadget especially firm and strong.

W.E.

1 Place the poles one on top of the other in the shape of an 'X'. Tie a Timber Hitch (see page 32) round both poles leaving a good length of cord on the working end.

2 Take the working end firmly round the poles three times, laying the cord neatly side by side and working the standing end into the lashing.

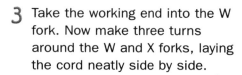

3 Take the working end into the W fork. Now make three turns around the W and X forks, laying the cord neatly side by side.

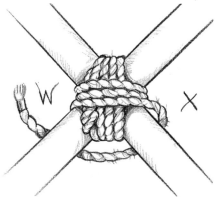

4 Take the working end and make three frapping turns between the poles to tighten the lashing. Finish off with a Clove Hitch (see page 37). Tuck in or trim the end.

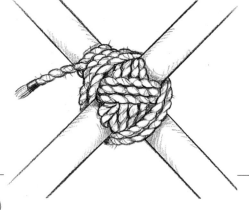

Sheer-Leg Lashing

This is used for joining two parallel poles, either to extend the length or to form an 'A' frame, as might be used in a pioneering project (see page 125).

1 Place the poles parallel to each other and tie a Clove Hitch (see page 37) around one pole.

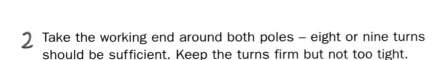

2 Take the working end around both poles – eight or nine turns should be sufficient. Keep the turns firm but not too tight.

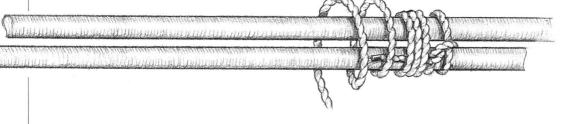

3 Take the working end and frap two or three times between the poles to secure the lashing. Keep the frapping firm. Finish off with a Clove Hitch (see page 37) tied closely to the end of the lashing.

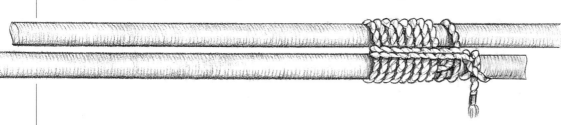

continued...

4 Where Sheer-Leg Lashing is used to extend the length of the poles it may be safer to have two lashings. If the poles still wobble despite a really firm lashing then a wedge can be placed into the lashing to make it more secure – put the wedge in from the top down.

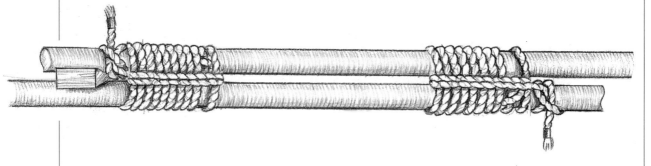

5 Where Sheer-Leg Lashing is used to make an 'A' frame use only one set of lashing. Start with the base of the pole level, so that the legs of the structure are equal. If using heavier poles, support the end you are working on with another pole. This will lift the poles clear of the ground and give easy access. Opening the legs into the 'A' shape will tighten the lashing.

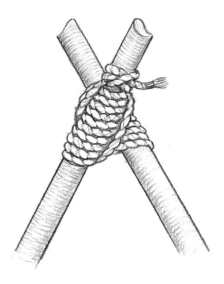

Camp Gadgets

Introduction

Now you can successfully tie knots and lashings, you can go on to making bigger things – gadgets. Gadgets can add a touch of luxury to any camp. They are great fun and very simple to make. All you need is thin rope or thick string for the lashings and a variety of lengths and thicknesses of wood. All the knots and lashings needed to construct these simple gadgets are featured in this book.

Detailed information on equipment needed for gadget-making can be found in *Camps and Holidays*.

Although gadgets are fun to make they must be safe, so the following points need to be considered:

- Everyone involved in building the gadget should know exactly what they are doing.
- Always make sure you use the best materials available. All the equipment you need is listed for each project. Remember to take along a mallet for hitting upright supports into the ground.
- Although there is no right or wrong way to make gadgets, it is important that they are strong, safe and serve the purpose. Always check the strength and stability of a gadget before using it. A good test is to try pushing the gadget to make sure it will stand up. Remember it should remain standing firmly whatever the weather.
- Make sure there are no sharp ends on gadgets as they could injure people and damage other equipment.

Once you have mastered the gadgets in this section, why not have a go at designing your own!

Traditional Flagpole

Make a basic flagpole for camp or Patrol base using Square Lashing (page 105), West Country Whipping (page 102) and Clove Hitches (page 37).

You need:

- 2 or 3 uprights such as broom sticks or Scout staves (the number depends on the height required)
- light cord for lashings
- 2 lengths of heavier cord or light rope for guy ropes
- 4 pegs
- 1 piece of wood for the cleat (about 300mm long)
- 1 ring or cord grommet
- 1 length of cord for the halyards
- 1 flag

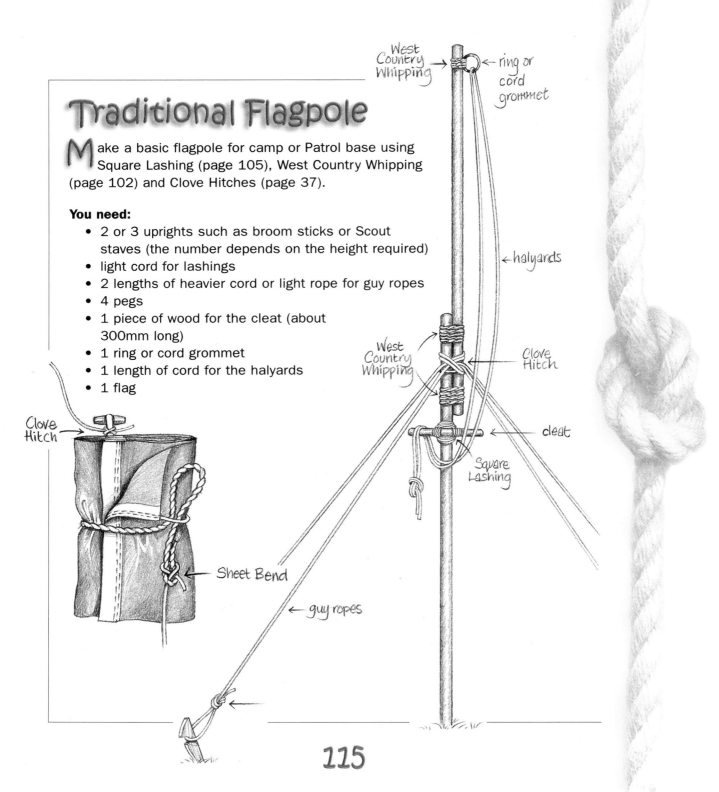

West Country Whipping

ring or cord grommet

halyards

West Country Whipping

Clove Hitch

cleat

Square Lashing

Clove Hitch

Sheet Bend

guy ropes

Patrol Camp Dresser

Using Diagonal Lashing (page 110), Square Lashing (page 105), Snake Lashing (page 107) and West Country Whipping (page 102) hang up your tea-towels and kitchen utensils on this Patrol camp dresser.

You need:
- 2 uprights
- 9 horizontal or crossing poles
- short sticks for table-top
- light cord for lashings
- 2 forked uprights (shorter than the two back uprights)
- 1 flag

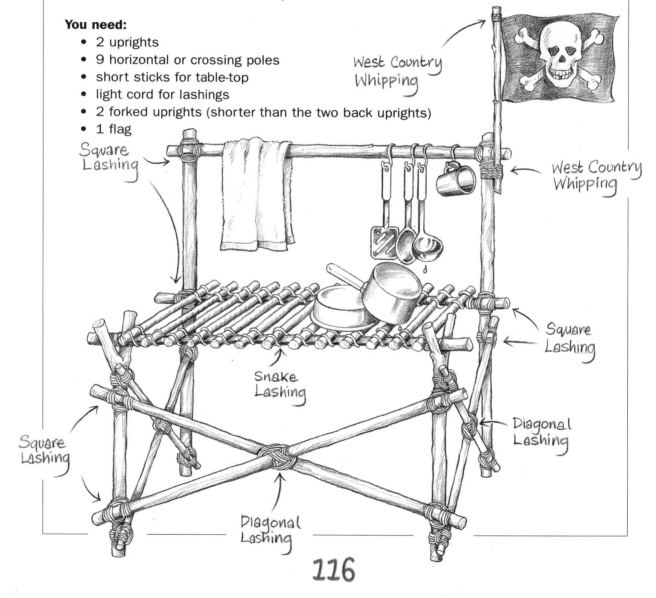

West Country Whipping

Square Lashing

West Country Whipping

Square Lashing

Snake Lashing

Diagonal Lashing

Square Lashing

Diagonal Lashing

Washstand

With Tripod Lashing (page 108), Square Lashing (page 105) and Snake Lashing (page 107) you can make a simple washstand.

You need:

- 3 uprights such as broom sticks or Scout staves
- 3 sticks for cross struts
- 4 or 5 sticks for the shelf
- light cord for lashings
- 1 washing-up bowl

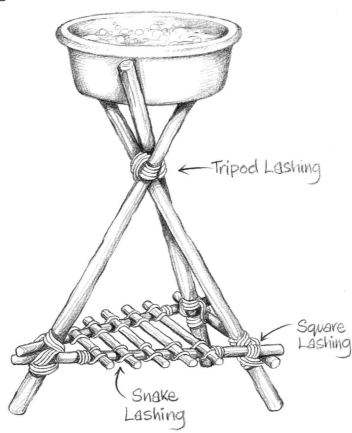

Tripod Lashing

Square Lashing

Snake Lashing

Gateway

U sing Tripod Lashing (page 108), Square Lashing (page 105) and a bit of imagination you can build a gateway that is sure to make a dramatic entrance to your camp!

You need:

- 6 x 4m poles (60–80mm in diameter)
- 6 x 2m short spars (40mm in diameter)
- 1 cross spar of similar weight, the length will depend on the width of the gateway
- 2 lengths of heavier cord or light rope for guy ropes
- light cord for lashings
- bunting

Tripod Lashing

Clove Hitch

guy ropes

Double Overhand Loop

Square Lashing

Pioneering

Introduction

Pioneering is fun but also requires great teamwork! A project will only be a success if the team works well together. So when planning a pioneering project try to make sure that everyone can take part in the preparation. It is not much fun standing around watching other people make something for 'you to play on'.

Start by tackling some of the smaller projects. Once you have built up your confidence, you can then move on to the more complex ones. Before you begin, make sure you can tie the following knots:

Clove Hitch – to put onto a closed or open spar (pages 37–8)
Round Turn and Two Half Hitches (page 25).

Materials

- Have a variety of lengths of wood available. Spars and poles can be obtained at a reasonable price from the Forestry Commission. For most pioneering projects you need 2.5–3m poles of about 100mm diameter. If you cannot obtain any wood, broom handles are great for practising with!
- Don't throw away those short pieces of wood. They will come in useful as pegs, pickets, ladder rungs and short crosspieces. You never know what might come in useful!
- Have a variety of ropes and lashings available. You can use natural or synthetic ropes but remember, unless well cared for, natural ropes have a tendency to rot (see page 139 for further details on looking after rope). In addition, synthetic ropes are more elastic and tend to stretch which may be a problem when making a bridge.
- Make a collection of old canvas, sacking and plastic fertiliser bags. These are very handy for protecting trees and your rope, and for making 'comfortable' seats.
- You will need a few handy tools: a hand axe, saw, a mallet, a lump hammer to deal with pickets, a spade and a knife. Remember to always take care when using tools.

Safety points

- Check spars are not rotten by striking with a mallet. A good pole sounds resonant, a rotten one dull and dead. Practise on spars that you know are good and rotten so that you can get used to the sound you should expect to hear.
- Check ropes for visible defects such as fraying, cuts, etc. If using natural ropes open the strands and look and smell for mould. If using man-made ropes, open strands and look for powder-like deposits. These ropes suffer badly from abrasion and crushing.
- Ensure all spars are cleared away so nobody falls over them.
- Never throw a spar down onto the ground – it will snap easily.
- Nominate one person to check that all the lashings have been finished off correctly and are secure. A good tip to ensure your frapping is tight is to use a frapping tapper (a large tent peg). Each time you come to a corner, having pulled your rope round, beat it with the narrow edge of your tapper into the corner. You will be able to feel the slack taking up. Remember, frap it and tap it! To ensure your lashing is tight use a mallet. Take the loose end of the lashing round the handle of the mallet, push down on the handle and the lashing will tighten up. This will get a lashing tighter than the strongest person can by hand.
- Make sure everybody knows what to do and how to use the structure before getting on it.
- When taking the strain on ropes, it is a good idea to have a ready supply of gardening gloves. This is to avoid rope burns and to get a better grip on the rope so nobody lets go at the wrong time!
- If you use a tree as an anchorage, protect it with sacking or old canvas. This will also help to prevent your rope from chafing!

Swing Bridge or Haymaker Bridge

This easy-to-make Swing Bridge allows you to cross water without getting wet! Make sure you find a suitable spot to construct your bridge – ensuring there is enough room for pioneers to hold onto the supporting ropes so that the bridge is secure for a pioneer to swing across.

What to do

1 Lay your poles on the ground at right angles making sure that one side of the horizontal pole is longer than the other. The butt end of the horizontal pole should be about 500mm above the butt of the upright pole.

2 Tie a Clove Hitch (page 38) in the centre of the lashing rope. Attach this about 1m above the butt of the upright pole.

3 Attach the two free ends of the lashing to the horizontal pole, tying with Clove Hitches and securing with Half Hitches (page 24). There should be approximately 300–400mm of rope between the upright pole and the horizontal pole.

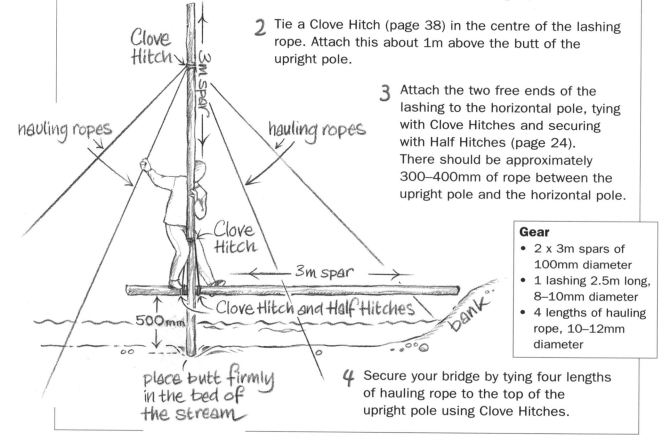

Clove Hitch

3m spar

hauling ropes

hauling ropes

Clove Hitch

3m spar

Clove Hitch and Half Hitches

bank

500mm

place butt firmly in the bed of the stream

Gear
- 2 x 3m spars of 100mm diameter
- 1 lashing 2.5m long, 8–10mm diameter
- 4 lengths of hauling rope, 10–12mm diameter

4 Secure your bridge by tying four lengths of hauling rope to the top of the upright pole using Clove Hitches.

How to use your Swing Bridge

The upright pole is placed firmly in the bed of the stream with the horizontal pole free to swing from one bank to the other. The upright pole is held vertically when the strain is taken on the four supporting ropes. The pioneer uses her balance to move the horizontal pole so she can get from one side of the bank to the other.

Rope Ladder

Although this seems a small pioneering project it is quite complicated as it requires you to know four knots – Double Overhand Knot (page 11), Sheet Bend (page 48), Marline Spike Hitch (page 46) and Round Turn and Two Half Hitches (page 25). It can be made and used indoors if you have a beamed ceiling.

Gear

- 1 rope about 15m long, 15–20mm diameter
- 1 rope about 7.5m long, 15–20mm diameter
- 15 rungs about 600mm long, 25mm diameter
- sacking or old canvas
- 2 pegs 400mm long

What to do

1 Lay the longest rope on the ground and divide in half. Tie a Double Overhand Knot (page 11) in the centre of the rope to form a loop.

2 Attach the shorter rope to the loop with a Sheet Bend (page 48).

3 Working down from the Double Overhand Knot make Marline Spike Hitches (page 46) on either side. Push a ladder rung through each bight you make. Ensure the hitches are level and there is not too much of a gap between the rungs, otherwise when the ladder is in use the ropes will stretch and you will not be able to step from rung to rung! It is also vital that the Marline Spike Hitches are the right way up or they will come undone when weight is put on the rung.

continued...

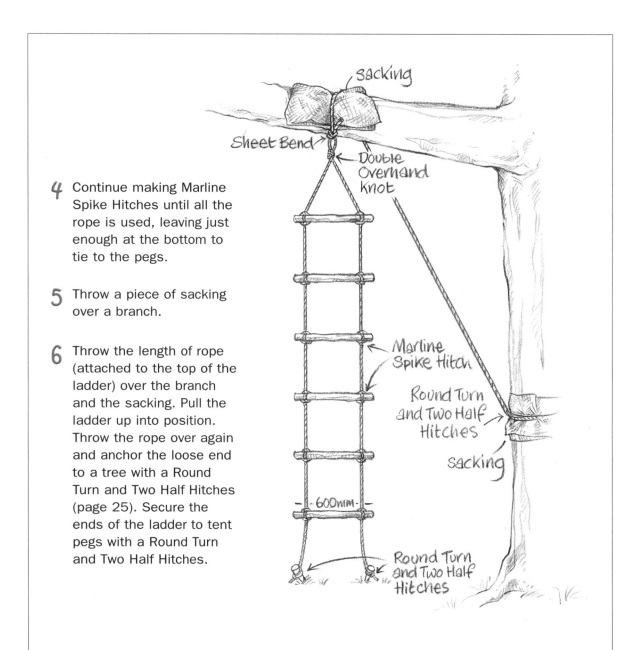

4 Continue making Marline Spike Hitches until all the rope is used, leaving just enough at the bottom to tie to the pegs.

5 Throw a piece of sacking over a branch.

6 Throw the length of rope (attached to the top of the ladder) over the branch and the sacking. Pull the ladder up into position. Throw the rope over again and anchor the loose end to a tree with a Round Turn and Two Half Hitches (page 25). Secure the ends of the ladder to tent pegs with a Round Turn and Two Half Hitches.

'A' Frame Transporter

The 'A' frame is a basic structure in pioneering and is extremely stable and strong. In pioneering a single 'A' frame is known as a pair of sheer-legs. This transporter can be used as a means of crossing a stream or gully.

What to do

1 Sheer Lash (page 111) the two longest poles together. The lashing should be about 1m down from the tip of the pole.

2 Open the sheer-legs to about 1.25m at the base. Square Lash (page 105) the 2m spar horizontally across the sheer-legs – about 450mm from the butt of the poles.

Gear

- sheer-legs:
  2 x 2.5m spars of 100mm diameter
  1 x 2m spar of 50mm diameter
  1 x 1m spar of 50mm diameter
- sacking or canvas
- 2 hauling ropes
- 1 lashing
  7.5m long,
  8–10mm diameter
- 4 lashings
  5.5m long,
  8–10mm diameter

rear ropes to take the strain

Clove Hitch

forward ropes for pulling

hessian padding for seat

Sheer Lashing

footrest

450mm

1m

2.5m spar

2.5m spar

Square Lashing

2m spar

450mm

3 Square Lash the 1m spar horizontally across the sheer-legs – about 450mm below the Sheer Lashing. This makes a good footrest.

4 Attach the hauling ropes. Middle each rope and tie a Clove Hitch (page 37) to the tip of each spar.

5 Tie sacking or canvas using sisal string around the sheer lashing to make a seat.

continued...

How to use your Transporter

Lay it on the ground with the legs in the water. A pioneer sits in the seat whilst four others 'man' the hauling ropes. The forward two ropes are pulled – some strength is needed here – perhaps two pioneers could help push the legs until the transporter is vertical. Now the two pioneers on the ropes at the rear take the strain and carefully let the traveller down on the other side.

Once you've mastered the technique of lowering someone safely, try transporting the whole team, one by one, from one side of the stream to the other. It can be done!

Swing or Trapeze

This is great fun to use but make sure you secure the base before you try it!
Test it gingerly! You'll hear one or two creaks and groans from the ropes and spars and there will be a slight movement of the sheer-legs.

What to do

1 Make two identical sets of sheer-legs (page 125) using the 3m spars. Sheer Lash them about 0.5m from the top of the spars, leaving enough space to fit in the crossbar.

2 Square Lash (page 105) a 2m spar horizontally across the sheer-legs – about 450mm from the butt of the poles.

3 Turn the sheer-legs on to their sides and put the crossbar into the crutch of the Sheer Lashing. Square Lash it to one of the uprights.

4 Attach a set of double guys to each spar. Do this by tying a Clove Hitch (page 38) in the centre of each guy and slipping it over the tip of the spar.

Gear

- sheer-legs:
  4 x 3m spars of 120mm diameter
  (It is important that the spars are 3–3.5m long. Any longer and you'll find them heavy and unwieldy, the trapeze will also tend to be unstable!)
  2 x 2m spars of 100mm diameter
- crossbar:
  1 x 2.1m spar of 100mm diameter preferably green or relatively recently cut as this spar will be bearing all your weight.
- seat:
  1 x 750mm spar of 75mm diameter
- sacking or canvas
- 4 sets of double guys
- 2 lashings 7.5m long
- 6 lashings 5.5m long
- 1 rope for the swing, 4.5m long
- 8 pickets

5 Attach the rope to the crossbar with a Clove Hitch. This will hold the seat of the swing.

6 Hoist into a vertical position, taking care that the project is kept square. Sink the butt ends into the ground to secure the structure. Set the guys at right angles to one another and secure to pickets with a Round Turn and Two Half Hitches (see page 25). Make sure that the pickets are firmly hammered into the ground. It's important here to make sure no-one is over zealous and pulls too hard on the guys, or the trapeze will topple over.

7 Secure the seat to the two ends of rope dangling from the crossbar, with a Round Turn and Two Half Hitches. For more comfort pad the seat with sacking or old canvas. Here you have a swing!

8 Shorten the ropes from the crossbar and you have a trapeze. Place the sheer-legs in a stream and you have a means of crossing it.

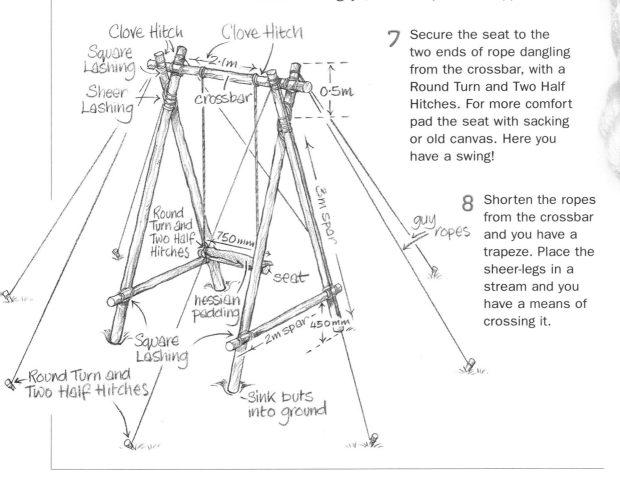

Clove Hitch   Clove Hitch
Square Lashing
Sheer Lashing
2.1m
crossbar
0.5m
Round Turn and Two Half Hitches
750mm
3m spar
guy ropes
seat
hessian padding
Square Lashing
2m spar   450mm
Round Turn and Two Half Hitches
sink butts into ground

Swingboat

A more challenging project but great fun to use when well constructed.

What to do

1 Make two sets of identical sheer-legs (page 125). The sheer lashing should be about 1m from the tips of the sheer-legs as this project has more overhead poles.

Round Turn and Two Half Hitches

Clove Hitch

2.1m spar →

Clove Hitch

Square Lashing

2m spar
2.1m spar

Square Lashing

Sheer Lashing

crossbar

3m spar

double guy ropes

Square Lashing

plank

Pulling rope

Clove Hitch and Half Hitches

sink buts into the ground

2.1m spar

Round Turn and Two Half Hitches

Gear
- sheer-legs:
  4 x 3–3.5m spars of 125mm diameter
  2 x 2m spars of 100mm diameter
  3 x 2.1m spars of 75mm diameter
- crossbar:
  1 x 2.1m spar of 125mm diameter, preferably green wood
- 1 plank for the seat
- 4 sets of double guys
- 4 lashings 7.5m long, 8–10mm diameter
- 6 lashings 5.5m long, 8–10mm diameter
- 4 lashings 6.5m long, 8–10mm diameter
- 2 ropes about 3.5m long, 20mm diameter, for attaching seat
- 2 ropes about 2.5m long, 8–10mm diameter, for pulling ropes
- 8 pickets

2 Turn the two sets of sheer-legs on their sides and Square Lash (page 105) the crossbar to the crutch of the sheer-legs. Square lash two more spars parallel to the crossbar to the front and back tips of the sheer-legs.

3 Middle the two ropes that will hold the seat and tie Clove Hitches (page 37) suitably spaced to the crossbar.

4 Turn the sheer-legs round to attach the top bar which will hold the pulling ropes. Square lash the top bar at right angles to the supporting bars.

5 Tie on the two pull ropes at either end of the spar with a Round Turn and Two Half Hitches (page 25).

6 Attach the set of double guys to the spars. Do this by tying a Clove Hitch (page 38) in the centre of each guy and slipping it over the tip of each spar.

7 Hoist into the vertical position. There will be four ends dangling from the crossbar. Attach each end of the seat to the rope with a Clove Hitch, locked with Half Hitches (page 24). Make sure the structure is secure by sinking the butt ends into the ground. Set the guys at right angles to one another and secure to pickets with a Round Turn and Two Half Hitches.

See-Saw

A fun piece of pioneering to use. However, make sure the roller and plank which are being used for the see-saw are sound and/or recently cut. These two pieces take all the weight.

Gear
- 4 x 3m spars of 125mm diameter
- 5 x 600mm spars of 100mm diameter
- plank or 1 x 3m spar of 125mm diameter
- roller
- 3 lashings 7.5m long, 8–10mm diameter
- 10 lashings 6.5m long, 8–10mm diameter
- 4 sets of double guy ropes
- 8 pickets

What to do

1 Make two identical sets of sheer-legs (page 125).

2 Turn the sheer-legs on their sides and Square Lash (page 105) a short crossbar across the crutches of the sheer-legs.

continued...

3 Square Lash four crosspieces to the legs, two on each side, about 600mm from the bottom of the spars, leaving sufficient space for the roller to be inserted between the spars. Use a piece of lashing rope to check that the crosspieces are level on both sides.

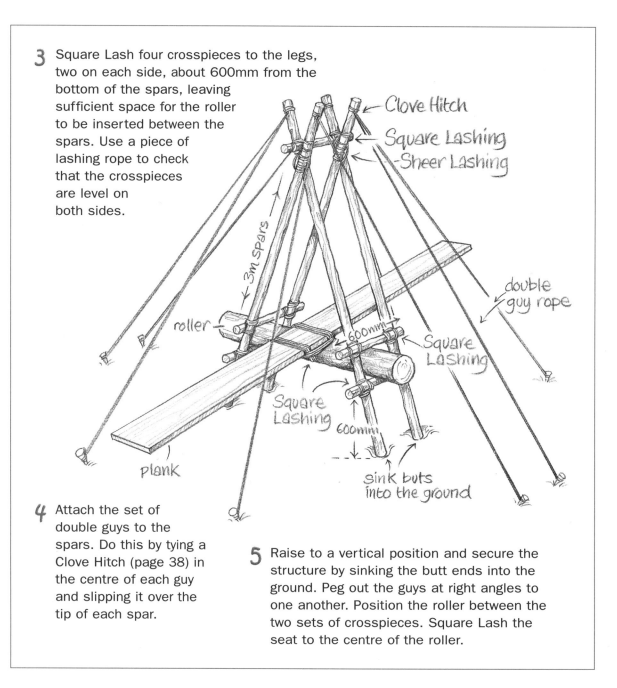

Clove Hitch

Square Lashing

Sheer Lashing

3m spars

roller

double guy rope

600mm

Square Lashing

plank

Square Lashing

600mm

sink buts into the ground

4 Attach the set of double guys to the spars. Do this by tying a Clove Hitch (page 38) in the centre of each guy and slipping it over the tip of each spar.

5 Raise to a vertical position and secure the structure by sinking the butt ends into the ground. Peg out the guys at right angles to one another. Position the roller between the two sets of crosspieces. Square Lash the seat to the centre of the roller.

Raft

How about pioneering afloat? A local pond would provide the ideal setting for a day's rafting. The fun is in testing your design — will it take your weight, or will it sink? Here's a basic design for a raft which will support just under 140kg so it will take two pioneers comfortably.

After one taste of rafting, you're sure to want to try again, to elaborate your design. What about a sail, a bigger raft to hold more pioneers, a streamlined design to race, or a raft regatta?

Gear

- 4 x 2.1m spars of 50mm diameter
- 4 x 1m spars of 50mm diameter
- 6 x 25 litres or 5 gallon drums
- 16 lashings 2.5m long, 8–10mm diameter
- 12 lashings 6m long, 8–10mm diameter

What to do

1 Lay the drums on their sides on the ground in a row of three. Lay a second row of drums in exactly the same way a metre away from the first row. Lay the four short poles lengthways between the drums.

2 Then taking one long pole at a time, place each pole vertically across the top of the drums and Square Lash (page 105) them to the short poles at the 16 crossing points.

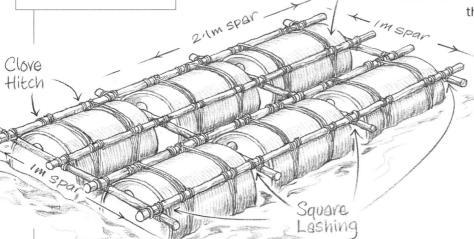

drums

2.1m spar

1m spar

Clove Hitch

1m spar

Square Lashing

continued...

3 Now you need to secure the drums to the frame. Begin with a Clove Hitch (page 37) on the spar. Take the working end over the drum and poles. Make three or four turns keeping the lashing as tight as you can. Finish with a Clove Hitch on a convenient spar. Repeat this to secure the other end of the drum to the poles. Continue this until all drums are firmly secured to the poles.

There is no specific method of fixing the drums, but here are some tips:
- Avoid using one length of lashing. Make two independent lashings so that if one does work loose, you still have a chance that the other will survive. Place the drums so that the stoppers will be above the surface of the water when the raft is in use.
- Don't use good ropes for lashings, as underwater chafing will ruin them. Use synthetic ropes which can be untied and dried out afterwards.

Safety points
- Before venturing afloat you must be able to swim 50m in clothes. Always make sure you wear a life jacket and trainers or canvas shoes.
- Ask your Guider to inspect your raft. The rules and conditions set out in *The Outdoor Manual* should be complied with.
- Treat your raft with care. Don't spoil all the hard work by dragging it over the ground and loosening all the lashings. Lift the raft into the water and don't sit on it until you are at least knee deep in water.
- Have a towing line attached at the back of your raft with a Round Turn and Two Half Hitches (page 25). If you do capsize or sink, don't panic, hold on to the raft and be towed back to shore.
- Ensure oil or plastic drums are clean. Oil and other chemicals and pesticides can pollute a pond and injure or kill wildlife.
- Know that you will get wet!

Sleeping Platform

Sleep under the stars on this pioneering platform. You could even try pitching your tent on top of the platform. It is up to you how high the platform is but please remember if people are sleeping on it that it must be secure. With this in mind, this project is probably better suited to the more experienced pioneer so they can select the height of the platform and the diameter of the spars according to how many people are sleeping on it. Alternatively the project can be overseen by someone familiar with equipment who can select suitable sizes.

Gear

- 9 spars of 75mm diameter for the tripods. (The length and diameter of the spars depends on how high from the ground you want your platform to be.)
- 3 x 3m spars of 125mm diameter
- spars of varying lengths to make the platform
- variety of ropes for lashings
- rope ladder if needed

What to do

1. Using Tripod Lashing (page 108) make three tripods with the lashings equal distance from the floor.

2. Position the tripods in a triangular formation. Sink the butt ends into the ground or secure with pegs especially if the structure is fairly high.

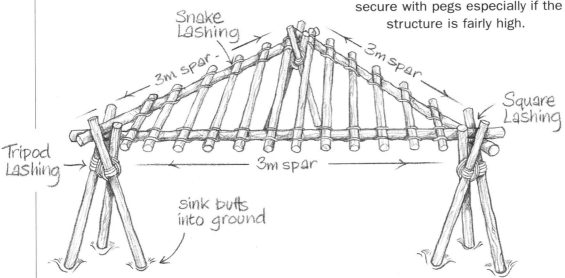

Snake Lashing

3m spar

3m spar

Square Lashing

3m spar

Tripod Lashing

sink butts into ground

continued...

3 Place the long spars between the tripods making sure the ends of the spars are on top of the Tripod Lashing. Square Lash (page 105) them in place.

4 Snake Lash (page 107) or Square Lash the assorted spars to the crosspoles to make the platform.

5 Attach a rope ladder if necessary.

6 In use you may need to belay yourself to the platform rather than roll off!

Skylon

This is used for securing a flagpole. Although this structure might look complicated, the only knot you need to know is the Clove Hitch (page 37).

1 Place the three spars in the ground at a central point.

2 Attach three guy ropes to the tip of each spar tying a Clove Hitch (page 37). Ease the spars apart so that the tips of the spars form an equilateral triangle.

3 Assemble the pegs into the ground ensuring they are an equal distance apart. Secure two of the guy ropes from each spar to the pegs tying a Clove Hitch.

4 Attach three guy ropes to the top of the flagpole tying a Clove Hitch.

5 Lift the flagpole up using the guy ropes as a steady and attach them to the tops of the three spars with a Clove Hitch.

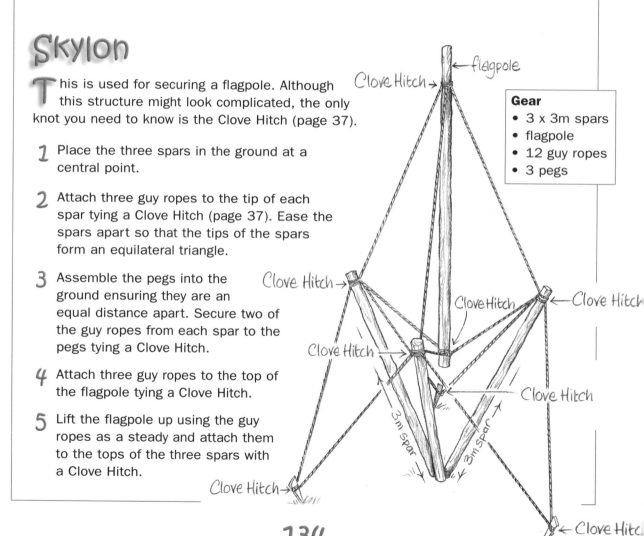

Gear
- 3 x 3m spars
- flagpole
- 12 guy ropes
- 3 pegs

6 Tie the third guy rope from each spar to the bottom of the flagpole with a Clove Hitch. Once all the guy ropes are tied, the weight of the flagpole will hold the structure together. Fine tune the structure by adjusting the Clove Hitches as necessary to get the Skylon symmetrical and upright.

Monkey Bridge or Burmah Bridge

The first task of any successful pioneer is to find the right site for the project in hand. In the case of the monkey bridge, a stream or gully with trees on either side would be ideal, failing the stream or gully, the trees will have to suffice, and without these you'll have to manage with home-made anchorages!

The preparatory work of building a monkey bridge falls into two sections:

a) the making of the sheer-legs

b) preparing the rope-way

Two groups of pioneers could be working on these at the same time.

Gear
- sheer-legs:
  4 x 3m spars of 125mm diameter
  2 x 2m spars of 50–75mm diameter
- extra crosspieces:
  2 x 1.5m spars of 75mm diameter
  2 x 1m spars of 75mm diameter
- sacking or old canvas
- 1 rope for main hawser (foot rope) about 20mm diameter
- 2 ropes for handrails about 20mm diameter
- 4 double guy ropes or 8 single, 8–10mm diameter
- 2 lashings 7.5m long, 8–10mm diameter
- 12 lashings 5.5m long, 8–10mm diameter
- Sisal string or synthetic rope
- At least 12 pickets
- 12 large pegs

What to do

1 Mark out the position of the sheer-legs, these should be exactly opposite and parallel to each other and no further apart than 13.7m. Make two sets of identical sheer-legs (page 125) – the Sheer Lashing must be at least 1.5m below the tip of the spars. This is to allow space for the rope-way.

2 Square Lash (page 105) the base pole to the sheer-legs about 300mm from the bottom of the spars. Square Lash two additional crosspieces on to the sheer-legs These act as steps and will help you climb on to the walkway.

continued...

3 Lash sacking or old canvas into the crutch of the sheer-legs, using sisal string to tie the material on. This reduces friction on the foot-rope as it lies in the sheer-legs.

4 Attach the set of double guys to the tips of the spars. Do this by tying a Clove Hitch (page 38) in the centre of each guy and slipping it over the top of each pole.

5 On flat ground lay out and peg the main foot-rope marking the distance between the sheer-legs and ensuring there is enough rope at each end for anchorages.

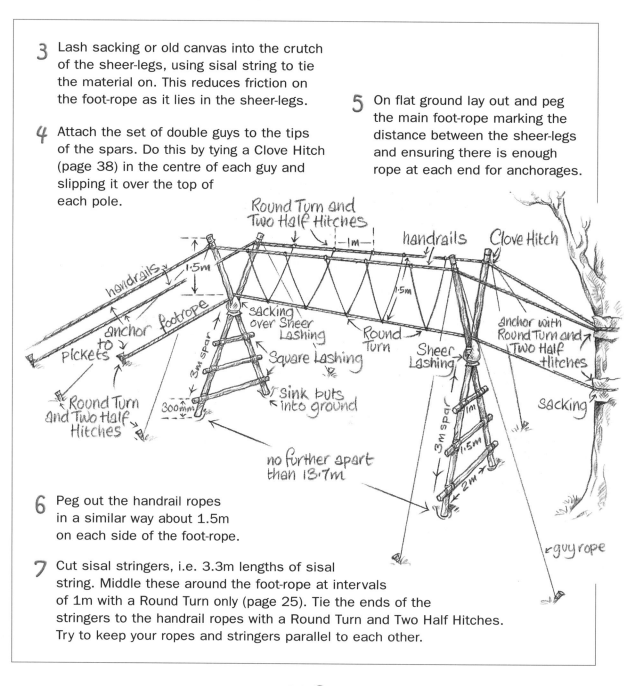

6 Peg out the handrail ropes in a similar way about 1.5m on each side of the foot-rope.

7 Cut sisal stringers, i.e. 3.3m lengths of sisal string. Middle these around the foot-rope at intervals of 1m with a Round Turn only (page 25). Tie the ends of the stringers to the handrail ropes with a Round Turn and Two Half Hitches. Try to keep your ropes and stringers parallel to each other.

8 Erect the sheer-legs in the position already decided in Step 1. Sink the butt ends into the ground to a depth of about 150mm. This will help to prevent the sheer-legs lifting or twisting when weight is put on the rope-way. For additional security you could peg the butts. Set the guys at right angles to one another and secure to pickets with a Round Turn and Two Half Hitches (page 25).

9 Mark the distance from the baseline of the sheer-legs to the front line of the anchorages. As a guide this should be three times the distance – ground to crutch of the sheer-legs. Pass the rope-way through the sheer-legs, hand strain the handrails and attach temporarily to the tips of the sheer-legs with a Clove Hitch.

10 Anchor the foot-rope on one side. Hand strain the other side of the foot-rope and anchor firmly to a tree or series of pickets on the opposite side with a Round Turn and Two Half Hitches. Remember to make sure that the foot-rope is in a straight line from one anchorage to the other.

11 Hand strain the handrails and attach to the tip of the sheer-legs with a locked Clove Hitch and anchored in the same way as the foot-rope. If pulleys are available a set of tackle will be useful to put some tension into it. Adjust the stringers so they are in line with one another to complete your bridge.

Ballista

This pioneering project is sure to create hours of fun. However, it can be quite tricky to get working properly and may require some patience! This project works well on a mini-pioneering scale using garden canes indoors.

What to do

1 Make a set of sheer-legs (page 125) using the two 3m poles. Square Lash (page 105) the two 1.5m spars to each side of the sheer-legs so that you now have three sets of sheer-legs joined together.

continued...

Gear
- sheer-legs:
  2 x 3m spars of
  100mm diameter
  2 x 1.5m spars of
  100mm diameter
- base:
  4 x 1m spars of
  100mm diameter
- 1 roller bar
- hessian or polythene
  padding
- firing arm:
  2 x 4.5m spars of
  100mm diameter
  4 x crosspoles
  colander for weapon
  holder
  heavy log for counter
  weight
- 4 x short crosspoles
  for stopper
- elastic
- pulling rope

2 Square Lash the four 1m spars across the base of the sheer-legs to secure the structure. Snake Lash (page 107) the four short crosspieces across the top of the sheer-legs to make a stopper.

3 Position roller bar so that it sits in the crutch of the two sheer-legs either side. Insert hessian and polythene padding under the roller bar.

4 Make a firing arm by Square Lashing two crosspoles at each end of the two 4.5m spars. One end holds your weapon holder and the other holds your counter weight.

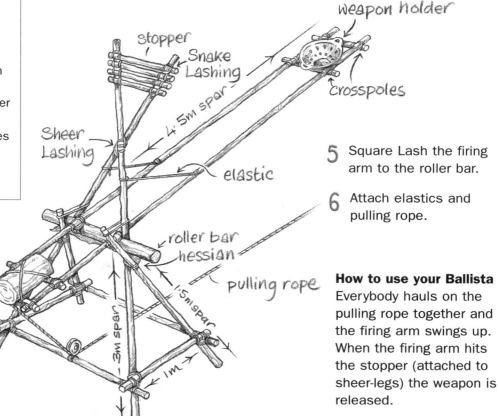

stopper · Snake Lashing · weapon holder · Crosspoles · 4.5m spar · Sheer Lashing · elastic · counter weight · Square Lashing · roller bar · hessian · 1.5m spar · pulling rope · 3m spar · 1m

5 Square Lash the firing arm to the roller bar.

6 Attach elastics and pulling rope.

How to use your Ballista
Everybody hauls on the pulling rope together and the firing arm swings up. When the firing arm hits the stopper (attached to sheer-legs) the weapon is released.

138

Caring for Your Materials

Whether you use rope, cord, or string your materials need to be looked after and stored carefully.

Checking your rope

Always examine the rope for knots or fraying. Run a complete length through your hands checking it thoroughly. About every two metres twist the rope to open up the strands. Inspect the inner strands, looking to see that they are not powdery or mildewed. When using string for gadget work make sure it is not rotten and that it has not been put under too much stress.

Storage

When buying a new rope ask how it should be stored. Different types of rope and cord need different conditions so that they last as long as possible and remain safe to use.

In general, however, it is important that rope is hung up and stored in a clean, dry, well-ventilated place away from direct sunlight. If your rope gets wet, dry it either outdoors by laying it loosely coiled in a shady place or suspended indoors to dry naturally at an even temperature. If a natural rope is stored away even slightly damp there is a danger it will shrink.

Before storing your rope, it should be coiled, knotted into an easy hank or made into a simple plait. Be careful not to tie it up too tight.

Coiling

1 Lay one end of the rope across the palm of one hand, keeping the other end about 450mm long.

2 With end B coil the rope across your hand. Bend end B back across your hand to form a loop.

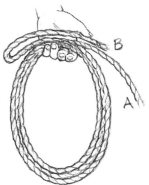

3 Take end A and whip it round loop X and the coil. Then take end A through X and pull end B to bring X down.

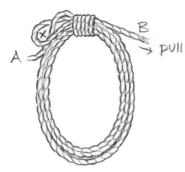

4 Tie off the ends to make a loop and hang the rope from this loop. Alternatively, if hanging the rope from a metal peg, put a strop – a circle of rope – through the loop or coil and hang it from this.

strop for hanging

Easy hank

1 Double the rope several times until it is about 400mm in length.

2 Secure by tying a Slip Knot (see page 21) in the rope.

3 When you want to use your rope again, pull on the working end and the cord will easily release.

→ pull to release

Simple Plait

Polypropylene ropes can be stored in a simple Chain Plait (see page 76).

Fraying

The ends of a piece of rope or cord are always likely to fray. Rope made from natural fibres such as hemp, sisal, flax and cotton can be whipped – a method of binding the end with string or twine. Refer to the section on Whippings (see page 100) for some examples. Splicing (see page 90) can also prevent fraying. Man-made ropes such as nylon, terylene and polypropylene will need to be heat sealed. This involves melting the ends of the rope with a match or candle flame. Remember to take extra care when doing this.

Points to remember

Provided you look after your rope properly, store it away correctly and do not put it under too much stress, there is no reason why your rope shouldn't remain safe for a good few years. Ropes do have a limited working life, however, those used in outdoor activities, including pioneering, should each have their own record book. This will ensure that anyone using the rope will know what it has been used for and when it will need to be replaced. You must always report if a rope has been put under extreme stress.

Usually a knot will untie quite easily, but once a knot has been put to use and had pressure put on it this may prove to be more difficult. Some knots have easy-release pulls built into them, but there are others whose purpose is to hold tightly – always. There may be times when you do have to cut a cord to prevent harm to another person or article, or perhaps in sheer despair of ever untying the tangle!

Glossary

Belay — Winding a rope around a fixture to make the rope fast.

Bend — Knot to join two cords.

A bight — A loop in the cord.

The bight — The length between the two ends of rope.

Brailing — Secures the bottom of a tent to prevent it from draughts and bellowing.

Butt — The heavy base-end of a spar or pole.

Cleat — A piece of wood or metal with two ends protruding used to fasten off a cord e.g. on a flagpole.

Cord — The general or generic term used in this book for cords, lines or thin rope.

Cordage — A comprehensive word for rope in general.

Core — The centre or heart of a rope or sennit.

Crowning — A knot of a number of strands in which each strand in regular turn passes over an adjacent strand and under the bight of another.

Doubled cords — Folding the cord in half so you work with two cords.

Frapping — The last turns on a lashing – usually at right angles to the other turns – to tighten the lashing.

Grommet — A rope ring.

Guy ropes — The cords or ropes supporting a vertical pole or structure.

Halyard — A light cord used for raising a flag.

Heel — The butt-end of a spar.

Heel-in — Sink the butt-end into the ground.

Hitch — Knot used to fasten a cord to another cord or object.

Knot — Anything that is deliberately tied in a cord or rope.

Lanyard — Cordage often braided and ornamental attached to knives, whistles and other personal items of equipment to prevent their loss.

Lash — Fastening or binding of two poles securely together.

Lay of the rope — The direction (either left-handed or right-handed) of twist in the strands of rope. Also the nature (tight, medium, loose) of that twist.

Loop — A part of the rope bent so that its parts come together or actually cross.

Macramé — The art of knotting cord or string in patterns to make decorative articles.

Make fast — Securing of a rope so that it stays firm when put under pressure.

Middle the rope Finding the centre of a rope or cord by folding it into two equal parts.

Natural rope Cordage of all kinds made from vegetable fibres.

Pegging butts Securing the butt-ends of a stave or pole into the ground with pegs.

Picket Pointed stake made of wood or metal.

Plait A sennit using three or more interlaced strands.

Release (of a knot) Simple untying of a knot.

Rope Any cordage over 10mm diameter.

Sennit Braided cordage in flat, round or square form made from three to nine cords.

Spar A pole or length of timber of varying sizes.

Splice To secure two ropes or two parts of the same rope together by interweaving the strands.

Standing end The fixed or non-moving end of a rope which might already be tied to another object.

Standing part The part of the rope which is not being used.

Stopper knot i) A knot tied to stop a threaded cord running out through a hole or cleat. ii) A secondary knot tied with a working end to prevent it running back through the initial knot when put under pressure.

Strand (of a rope) Two or more yarns twisted together.

String Thick thread, twine, thin cordage usually for domestic use.

Synthetic rope Cordage made from man-made fibres.

Thread A yarn.

Tip Top of a spar or pole.

Twine A fine string used for whipping ends of a rope.

Tying on Attaching or tying a rope to another object.

Whipping Binding at the end of a rope to stop it fraying.

Woggle A ring made from leather, cord, etc through which the ends of a neckerchief are passed at the neck.

Work a knot To shape a knot neatly.

Working end The end of the rope with which the knot is tied.

Working part The part of the rope with which you are tying the knot.

Further Reading

The following list outlines a selection of resources which may be helpful to the knotter.

Internal resources published by The Guide Association
- *A World of Ideas,* Trading Service ordering code 63867
- *Camps and Holidays,* Trading Service ordering code 63396
- *Knots for Everybody/Whippings and Lashings,* Trading Service ordering code 60731

The above publications are all available from the Association's Trading Service, Guide shops and depots. Contact The Guide Association Trading Service, Atlantic Street, Broadheath, Altrincham, Cheshire WA14 5EQ. Tel: 0161–941 2237 Fax: 0161–941 6326

External resources available through The Guide Association
- *The Alternative Knot Book* by Dr Harry Asher, published by Adlard Coles Nautical (1989), Trading Service ordering code 72157
- *The Knot Book* by Geoffrey Budworth, published by Elliot Right Way Books (1997), Trading Service ordering code 74518
- *Knots and Splices* by Jeff Toghill, published by Fernhurst Books (1979), Trading Service ordering code 74682

The above publications are all available from the Association's Trading Service, Guide shops and depots. For contact details, see above.

External resources available from all good bookshops
- *The Ashley Book of Knots* by Clifford W Ashley, published by Faber and Faber (1993)
- *Knots, Ties and Splices* by Commander J Irving, published by Routledge & Kegan Paul Ltd (1934)
- *Learnabout... Knots* by Ronald A L Hinton, published by Ladybird Books Ltd (1977)
- *Scout Pioneering* by John Sweet, published by The Scout Association (1974)
- *You Can Do Thousands of Things with String* by David Miller, published by Allen & Unwin (1996)